## DATE DUE

OPPOSING VIEWPOINTS®

# TERMINAL ILLNESS

OPPOSING VIEWPOINTS ®

# TERMINAL ILLNESS

# Other Books of Related Interest

OPPOSING VIEWPOINTS®

# TERMINAL ILLNESS

Andrea C. Nakaya, *Book Editor*

Bruce Glassman, *Vice President*
Bonnie Szumski, *Publisher*
Helen Cothran, *Managing Editor*

OPPOSING
VIEWPOINTS®
SERIES

**GREENHAVEN PRESS**
*An imprint of Thomson Gale, a part of The Thomson Corporation*

THOMSON
———✳———™
GALE

Detroit • New York • San Francisco • San Diego • New Haven, Conn.
Waterville, Maine • London • Munich

**THOMSON**

—————✴——————™

**GALE**

*For more information, contact*
Greenhaven Press
27500 Drake Rd.
Farmington Hills, MI 48331-3535
Or you can visit our Internet site at http://www.gale.com

Cover credit: © RubberBall

**LIBRARY OF CONGRESS CATALOGING-IN-PUBLICATION DATA**

Terminal illness : opposing viewpoints / Andrea C. Nakaya, book editor.
    p. cm. — (Opposing viewpoints series)
  Previously published in 2001 / edited by Mary E. Williams
  Includes bibliographical references and index.
  ISBN 0-7377-2963-5 (lib. : alk. paper) — ISBN 0-7377-2964-3 (pbk. : alk. paper)
    1. Terminal care. 2. Palliative treatment. 3. Euthanasia. I. Nakaya, Andrea C.,
  1976– . II. Opposing viewpoints series (Unnumbered)
  R726.8.T4646 2005
  362.17'5—dc22                                                    2004060595

Printed in the United States of America

"Congress shall make no law...abridging the freedom of speech, or of the press."

*First Amendment to the U.S. Constitution*

The basic foundation of our democracy is the First Amendment guarantee of freedom of expression. The Opposing Viewpoints Series is dedicated to the concept of this basic freedom and the idea that it is more important to practice it than to enshrine it.

# Contents

**Chapter 3: How Can the Spiritual and Emotional
Pain of Terminal Illness Be Eased?**

# Why Consider Opposing Viewpoints?

*"The only way in which a human being can make some approach to knowing the whole of a subject is by hearing what can be said about it by persons of every variety of opinion and studying all modes in which it can be looked at by every character of mind. No wise man ever acquired his wisdom in any mode but this."*

John Stuart Mill

In our media-intensive culture it is not difficult to find differing opinions. Thousands of newspapers and magazines and dozens of radio and television talk shows resound with differing points of view. The difficulty lies in deciding which opinion to agree with and which "experts" seem the most credible. The more inundated we become with differing opinions and claims, the more essential it is to hone critical reading and thinking skills to evaluate these ideas. Opposing Viewpoints books address this problem directly by presenting stimulating debates that can be used to enhance and teach these skills. The varied opinions contained in each book examine many different aspects of a single issue. While examining these conveniently edited opposing views, readers can develop critical thinking skills such as the ability to compare and contrast authors' credibility, facts, argumentation styles, use of persuasive techniques, and other stylistic tools. In short, the Opposing Viewpoints Series is an ideal way to attain the higher-level thinking and reading skills so essential in a culture of diverse and contradictory opinions.

In addition to providing a tool for critical thinking, Opposing Viewpoints books challenge readers to question their own strongly held opinions and assumptions. Most people form their opinions on the basis of upbringing, peer pressure, and personal, cultural, or professional bias. By reading carefully balanced opposing views, readers must directly confront new ideas as well as the opinions of those with whom they disagree. This is not to simplistically argue that everyone who reads opposing views will—or should—change his or her opinion. Instead, the series enhances readers' understanding of their own views by encouraging confrontation with opposing ideas. Careful examination of others' views can lead to the readers' understanding of the logical inconsistencies in their own opinions, perspective on why they hold an opinion, and the consideration of the possibility that their opinion requires further evaluation.

## Evaluating Other Opinions

To ensure that this type of examination occurs, Opposing Viewpoints books present all types of opinions. Prominent spokespeople on different sides of each issue as well as well-known professionals from many disciplines challenge the reader. An additional goal of the series is to provide a forum for other, less known, or even unpopular viewpoints. The opinion of an ordinary person who has had to make the decision to cut off life support from a terminally ill relative, for example, may be just as valuable and provide just as much insight as a medical ethicist's professional opinion. The editors have two additional purposes in including these less known views. One, the editors encourage readers to respect others' opinions—even when not enhanced by professional credibility. It is only by reading or listening to and objectively evaluating others' ideas that one can determine whether they are worthy of consideration. Two, the inclusion of such viewpoints encourages the important critical thinking skill of objectively evaluating an author's credentials and bias. This evaluation will illuminate an author's reasons for taking a particular stance on an issue and will aid in readers' evaluation of the author's ideas.

It is our hope that these books will give readers a deeper understanding of the issues debated and an appreciation of the complexity of even seemingly simple issues when good and honest people disagree. This awareness is particularly important in a democratic society such as ours in which people enter into public debate to determine the common good. Those with whom one disagrees should not be regarded as enemies but rather as people whose views deserve careful examination and may shed light on one's own.

Thomas Jefferson once said that "difference of opinion leads to inquiry, and inquiry to truth." Jefferson, a broadly educated man, argued that "if a nation expects to be ignorant and free . . . it expects what never was and never will be." As individuals and as a nation, it is imperative that we consider the opinions of others and examine them with skill and discernment. The Opposing Viewpoints Series is intended to help readers achieve this goal.

David L. Bender and Bruno Leone,
Founders

---

Greenhaven Press anthologies primarily consist of previously published material taken from a variety of sources, including periodicals, books, scholarly journals, newspapers, government documents, and position papers from private and public organizations. These original sources are often edited for length and to ensure their accessibility for a young adult audience. The anthology editors also change the original titles of these works in order to clearly present the main thesis of each viewpoint and to explicitly indicate the opinion presented in the viewpoint. These alterations are made in consideration of both the reading and comprehension levels of a young adult audience. Every effort is made to ensure that Greenhaven Press accurately reflects the original intent of the authors included in this anthology.

---

# Introduction

*"Recent medical and technological advances have had tremendous benefit to patients, and society as a whole."*
—Rhode Island state law, declaration on human cloning, Title 23, Section 23-16.4-1

*"The medical establishment has become a major threat to health."*
—Ivan Illich, philosopher and social theorist

The iron lung, precursor to the modern ventilator machine, enables a person to breathe who otherwise could not by forcing oxygen into his or her lungs. During the 1950s it was used to save the lives of thousands of children whose throat and lung muscles had been paralyzed by polio. Before the invention of the iron lung, these children's conditions were considered terminal; unable to get oxygen into their lungs, they simply died. With breathing assistance from the iron lung, however, many did not die. Some used the machine during the worst phase of the disease and later regained the use of their breathing muscles. Some used it only at night, while others used the machine for the rest of their lives. The invention of the iron lung meant that for many patients, polio was no longer a death sentence.

In "Looking Back on the Millennium in Medicine," a 2000 article published by the *New England Journal of Medicine*, the editors examine inventions such as the iron lung and conclude, "It is hard not to be moved by the astounding course of medical history over the past thousand years. No one alive in the year 1000 could possibly have imagined what was in store." Artificial respiration is only one example of how astounding medical advances are allowing patients to live with, and even recover from, illnesses that were once considered terminal. Throughout history, medical technology has advanced, and in the process it has changed the definition of terminal illness.

As a result of new medical innovations, people now live far longer than they did a hundred years ago, and when death comes, it is often anticipated for months or even years in advance. In *Suicide and Attempted Suicide*, author Geo Stone discusses dying in America to show how death in developed nations has changed drastically over the last century. According to him, in 1900 the life expectancy in the United States was forty-seven years, while by the mid-1990s it had risen to seventy-seven. In earlier times people typically died quickly from infectious disease or infections following injury, Stone claims, whereas now most Americans die from degenerative diseases such as heart disease, diabetes, stroke, and cancer. Today, 70 to 80 percent of the U.S. population will die of illnesses that they have had for months or even years, concludes Stone. Author John Hardwig echoes Stone's belief that dying in America is a lengthier process than it used to be. "Once, people normally got sick and died in a matter of days or weeks," says Hardwig. "Now the average American will know three years in advance what she will die of."

Many people believe that the increased ability to evade death has had a negative effect on the process of dying from a terminal illness. They argue that because the medical profession puts a focus on preventing death above all else it ignores the dying process. They claim that the medical community rarely helps patients to enjoy a good quality of life while dying, or to die a peaceful death. According to Doctor Zail Berry, "The medical complex has created this terrible monster, the idea that we can prevent death, that we can avoid it altogether. . . . But everybody dies at some point. . . . Life is fatal." Physicians Lofty L. Basta and Henry D. McIntosh discuss the effect of trying to evade the inevitability of death. In their opinion, a quick death is sometimes better than one artificially prolonged by technology. "Aside from the staggering increase in cost(s) for medical care," they allege, "a quick, painless death . . . has been replaced by a protracted last chapter of life, often with a mindless existence or hopelessly deteriorating bodily functions. For many, such existence robs them of much treasured dignity and valued richness of living." In *French Journal*, Horatio C. Wood IV discusses this type of death, which he calls the "wild death," where the sick no longer die naturally and peacefully but instead spend their last days fearful and unhappy as doctors invade their bodies with technology. According to Wood:

> In the past, prior to advances in medicine—before anesthesia, antibiotics, electrocardiograms, x-rays, intravenous fluids, oxygen machines, CAT scans, MRIs—death was natural. The French historian Phillippe Aries characterized a death taking place in those times as a "tame death." We have definitely lost that. . . . Modern medicine has done a job with its striking transformation of mortality. But its beneficence has been at a terrible price: the tame death has disappeared and the wild death has come into being.

However, while arguments such as Wood's are prevalent, there are also many people who applaud the way medical technology has prolonged life. According to John P. Bunker of the London Medical School, people now live richer lives because of the way that the medical field strives to defeat death. He writes, "The years of improved physical or mental function, or of prevention or amelioration of pain and suffering, add up to an estimated 500 per 100 individuals. That is, about 5 years on average per individual." Physician Joseph Calfee also defends lifesaving advances in medicine as greatly beneficial to society. By focusing on the negative aspects of end-of-life care, he argues, "we can often lose sight of the 'big-picture.'" He adds, "Medical progress brings benefits to society, including increased productivity, decreased mortality, and improved human health. As a result, it is critical to remind ourselves that medical innovation has quantifiable benefits." Writer Ian Frazier also counters critics of new medical technology with his argument that not only should the medical field embrace these advances, it actually has a responsibility to continually fight death. "For centuries we've accepted the myth of life as a 'natural' cycle, with a beginning, a middle, and an end, conveniently overlooking our own responsibility in it," he maintains. Frazier believes that society should not accept the inevitability of death and should continually strive to extend life.

Terminal illness is an emotionally-charged subject that affects large numbers of people every year. The way medical technology has prolonged life and changed death is one of many issues debated in discussions about terminal illness. The authors in this anthology offer differing views on other conflicts provoked by this controversial topic in the following chapters: Do the Terminally Ill Receive Quality End-of-Life Care? How Should the Physical Pain of Terminal Illness Be Relieved? How Can the Spiritual and Emotional Pain of Terminal Illness Be Eased? and Should Euthanasia Be Allowed for Terminally Ill Patients? To be sure, the increasing likelihood that individuals will die after a long illness has spurred interest in this controversial topic.

# CHAPTER 1

# Do the Terminally Ill Receive Quality End-of-Life Care?

# Chapter Preface

In 2002 the Partnership to Improve End-of-Life Care in Utah surveyed people who had recently lost a loved one; the purpose of the survey was to see whether the wishes of the dying were being followed. It found that most people, given a choice, would like to die at home. Dying at home was seen by many as a way to achieve a more peaceful death than they would likely experience in a hospital. Marilyn Woodward told the researchers about her husband Grant, who was suffering from chronic heart failure. He was able to achieve a "peaceful" and "beautiful" death because he was at home, surrounded by his family, she said. However, while the survey found that many people such as Grant Woodward wanted to spend the end of their lives at home, it also revealed that in many cases, this was not what happened. The frequency with which patients' wishes to die at home are honored is one measurement of the quality of care dying people receive in America.

The Utah study's findings are not unique. According to a nationwide study conducted by Last Acts, a national coalition that works to improve care for the dying, while the majority of Americans wish to die at home, in reality few do. Due to advances in medicine, people are increasingly dying in hospitals, where a series of technologies are employed to prolong life. According to author David Kessler, "Modern medicine is still over-treating most patients; trying for a cure when a cure is no longer possible." He laments the fact that the majority of Americans wish to die peacefully at home yet usually end up in a hospital, with doctors "trying to the end to save their lives." This, states Kessler, does not constitute dying well.

However, there are also many people who argue that dying in America is improving, with more patients' wishes being followed. Rick Weiss, writing in the *Washington Post*, argues that more Americans now die at home or in hospice care. According to Weiss, researchers at the National Institutes of Health scanned 35.2 million death certificates from 1980 to 1998 and found that during that period, the proportion of patients dying as hospital inpatients dropped from 54 percent to 41 percent. Editor Bill Berlow also believes that the death experience for the terminally ill is improving. "For decades," he says, "with the advent of miracle drugs and even more miraculous technology, the duel with death has often kept terminally ill patients—and those keeping vigil—in hospitals, nursing homes and other care facilities. But more and more often, when there's nothing left to be done but to manage the pain, patients and their families are choosing to die at home."

As the debate over dying at home illustrates, there is widespread disagreement about whether terminally ill patients receive adequate care in the United States. While some people argue that the U.S. health care system offers quality end-of-life care, others contend that it prevents terminally ill patients from experiencing a good death. The authors in the following chapter examine some of the issues related to care of the terminally ill in the United States.

*"[The baby boomer] generation is already preoccupied with dying a 'good death,' and they're willing to hire experts to help them achieve this."*

# Americans Are Increasingly Well Informed About How to Obtain Quality End-of-Life Care

Lisa Miller

Many Americans are dissatisfied with the death experience associated with hospitals and funeral homes, writes Lisa Miller in the following viewpoint. According to her, increasing numbers of people are planning in advance for their deaths in an attempt to make the dying experience less frightening. A large number of new businesses have been created, says Miller, that help people achieve this desire for more control over their deaths. Miller is a staff reporter for the *Wall Street Journal*.

As you read, consider the following questions:

1. According to the author, why are baby boomers preoccupied with dying a "good death"?
2. In Miller's opinion, what are the two great fears of dying people?
3. Why is Michael Krim an exception to most death consultants, according to the author?

In a converted garage here [in Sebastopol, California], a new service industry is being born. Call it personal consultants for death.

Jerri Lyons is explaining to the dozen people gathered for a workshop in her tiny office-apartment that when they or their loved ones die, they don't have to call a funeral home. If they engage the services of her business, Home Funeral Ministry, Ms. Lyons will help them care for and memorialize their deceased at home: She'll help dying people make future arrangements for their plants or pets. She'll instruct friends and family members in how to fill out a death certificate. She'll deliver the cardboard casket needed for cremation, or recommend a casket purveyor.

Ms. Lyons helps people achieve the kind of death and funeral they envision. "I take care of what needs to be taken care of," says Ms. Lyons, who is 52. "It's like planning a wedding or anything else." Since Ms. Lyons started her business four years ago [in 1996], she has helped 130 families with home deaths and funerals.

Home Funeral Ministry is part of a tiny but growing group of consultants who offer a new approach to the end of life. Convinced that the funeral industry, organized religion and the medical establishment fail to provide spiritual, fulfilling or intimate deaths, these professionals are stepping in to fill the void.

Here in Northern California, where many alternative movements are born, the death-guide industry is taking hold. Some practitioners operate like professional best friends, offering a sympathetic ear, practical advice and assurance that they will be there at the end. Others act more like clerics, helping people solve family problems. Another group, which includes Ms. Lyons, shepherds families through home death and memorial services, much as midwives did with natural and home childbirth in the 1970s.

In their fifties now, the baby boomers are thinking about mortality. Just as they revised their parents' vision of "the good life," insisting on spiritual and emotional health as well as material success, this generation is already preoccupied with dying a "good death," and they're willing to hire experts to help them achieve this.

Baby boomers have "written their own wedding vows," says Lisa Carlson, executive director of Funeral Consumers Alliance, in Hinesburg, Vt. Just as they've rediscovered breast feeding and home schooling, "now they want to personalize and take control of the death experience as well."

The ideal of a spiritual or "good" death is taking root in mainstream culture. Since 1994, hedge-fund manager George Soros has given $30 million to his Project on Death in America, which supports research projects that aim to alleviate the "physical, emotional, existential and spiritual" suffering of death.

## Bill Moyers Special

In September [2000], PBS will air a four-part series on death with Bill Moyers, which includes topics such as getting your spiritual life in order before you die.

"The Tibetan Book of Living and Dying," which describes death as a transition more than an end, has sold 50,000 copies every year since its publication in 1993, and a new book, Kathleen Dowling Singh's "The Grace in Dying," is being hailed as an updated, more spiritual version of [psychiatrist] Elisabeth Kübler-Ross's classic "On Death and Dying."

More people are teaching and taking classes on improving the experience of death. Medical schools and hospitals are beginning to train doctors about the non-clinical aspects of dying. From Duke University to the University of California at Santa Cruz, educational institutions are holding symposiums that talk about such topics as spiritual death, virtuous death, life after death and personally preparing for death.

## "Mentors Through Dying"

Three years ago [in 1997], Frank Ostaseski, founder of the Zen Hospice in San Francisco, developed a two-day, $150 workshop called "Facing Death: Being a Compassionate Companion," and 200 people signed up. Last year [1999], 2,500 people did. Next year, Mr. Ostaseski plans to launch a certification program for professional death companions. Graduates will be called something like "midwives for death" or "mentors through dying."

The death-guide profession is still in its infancy, however.

Its practitioners carry no special credentials and their fees vary as widely as their techniques. Patrick Thornton steps in months, or even years, before death. He charges a basic rate of $140 per 90-minute session to dying clients in his practice based in Santa Rosa, Calif. In the sessions, Mr. Thornton uses yoga and Buddhist meditation techniques to help people face fear and pain.

The Chalice of Repose Project Inc., on the other hand, sends classical harpists and vocalists at no charge to people as they are dying. Ancient, sacred tunes provide relief from fear and suffering, the Missoula, Mont., nonprofit says.

Similarly, Megory Anderson charges nothing for her service: custom-made deathbed rituals. Ms. Anderson, formerly an Anglican nun, will read from sacred texts, anoint with oil, light candles and say prayers suited to the dying person's cultural and religious background. Since 1994, she has sat with nearly 200 people—and their families—as they died. In lieu of payment, she accepts donations to her Sacred Dying Foundation in San Francisco.

These practitioners didn't invent the idea of quality death, of course. In the 1970s, the hospice concept revolutionized the end of life by assisting dying people, mostly at home, with pain management and other quality-of-life issues. But some feel that the modern hospice, as it grows into a mature industry dependent on government dollars, has become too institutional.

Hospice has "lost its spiritual roots," says Dale Borglum, executive director of the Living/Dying Project in Fairfax, Calif., which trains volunteers to give spiritual support to the dying.

## "Nobody Died in Private"

For ages, dying happened at home. Family and clergy were close at hand to minister to the dying person's practical and spiritual needs. In the old days, "nobody died in private," says Robert Burt, law professor at Yale University, who is on the advisory board of the Project on Death in America. "Everybody trooped in the deathbed room. And the higher your class, the more people you had in the room."

But by the 1950s, most deaths occurred in the hospital.

More than 70% of Americans now die in a hospital or other institution, and the vast majority, once dead, are cared for by funeral homes. Relieved of their traditional responsibilities, family members have grown increasingly removed from their dying and their dead. And as ties to organized religion loosen, the cleric's role has diminished as well.

Nobleman. © 2002 by the *Spectator*. Reproduced by permission of Marc Tyler Nobleman.

Today, dying people have two great fears. The first is physical pain, and the second is dying alone. The latter fear is well-founded. Over the next 10 years, the number of people older than 65 and living alone in America will rise nearly 10% to more than 10 million, according to U.S. Census Bureau projections.

## Inner Lives

With the breakdown of family and social-support systems, dying alone "is much more prevalent than it has ever been," says Betsy MacGregor, a physician at Beth Israel Medical Center in New York, who has a grant to study the inner lives of people who are dying. Yet the primal yearning of the dying to make human connections is as strong as ever, she says.

Dying is dying, of course, and it is often far from tranquil. Mr. Burt of the Project on Death in America, warns against over-idealizing beautiful death and the people who claim to deliver it: "I'm all for the idea of a good death . . . of peace and grace and spiritual transcendence," he says. "But when you're dealing with the symptoms of pain and vomiting, that's not easy to do."

But more and more people are seeking practical and existential companionship as they die. Earlier this month [February 2000], David Gagat, who is 44, flew to Fairfax, Calif., from his home in Cleveland to attend a workshop called "Awakening the Healing Mind," given by Mr. Borglum. Mr. Gagat has amyotrophic lateral sclerosis, the terminal degenerative nerve and muscle disease also known as Lou Gehrig's disease. Divorced and living alone with physical therapists and caretakers, Mr. Gagat wanted to explore the nature of death more deeply. "Society isolates you when it comes to death," says Mr. Gagat, formerly an oil-company executive. "It's like people don't want to talk about it."

Sitting in a semicircle in front of a blazing fire, Mr. Gagat and the 20 other workshop participants introduce themselves. Several people want to be better companions to dying relatives. Neill Whitman, who is 75 and healthy, finds himself contemplating his own death—"my next great adventure," he says. "I don't want to go into it unprepared."

## "How Do You Want to Be Healed?"

During the workshop, Mr. Borglum describes what sages say death is like: a wondrous light, perhaps a loud noise, and then a melding with that light. He also teaches meditation techniques for being calm and compassionate in the face of death. In one exercise, pairs of participants face each other: No matter what one person says, the other can only respond with "How do you want to be healed?"

Participants in his workshops used to be "very young, and very experimental," says Mr. Borglum. Now, they "represent a cross section of middle America." Indeed, along with Messrs. Gagat and Whitman, attendees include a video producer and a woman who makes deliveries for Federal Express.

Some of the new death guides offer practical, rather than spiritual, help. On an unusually turbulent flight to London from Los Angeles last year [1999], Todd Michael Krim, who is 30, saw his life flash before his eyes and realized he hadn't properly said "I love you" to his family and friends.

So in September he launched FinalThoughts.com Inc., and since then about 5,000 people have signed up for the free service. FinalThoughts members store private messages to loved ones on the Web site and designate a special "Guardian Angel" to push the "send" button after they've died.

Then, last wishes and unexpressed sentiments travel via e-mail to their destinations. Also on the Web site: information on estate and funeral planning and organ donation. "We're basically going to be the one-stop shop for all end-of-life issues," says Mr. Krim. FinalThoughts.com recently received about $500,000 in seed capital and plans to generate revenue through advertisements, sponsorships and referrals.

But Mr. Krim is an exception. Most of the new death consultants operate on shoestring budgets. "We are just paying our bills," says Ms. Lyons of Home Funeral Ministry. "This is heart work." Ms. Lyons and her business partner, Janelle Va Melvin, run two death-consulting companies so small that together they made less than $30,000 last year. Revenues for Home Funeral Ministry come from donations— $350 for a cremation, $400 for a burial—and from extras. Home Funeral Ministry charges $35 for a cardboard cremation box; $18 for plans that describe how to build a plain pine casket; and 69 cents a pound for the dry ice that will preserve a body through a days-long wake.

Ms. Lyons's other business, the Natural Death Care Project [NDCP], is a division of a non-profit company concerned with environmental and end-of-life issues. NDCP does workshops and lectures, sells informational brochures and books, and consults with people interested in home funerals: at $60 for an initial consultation.

On this springlike January day, Ms. Lyons and Ms. Melvin are leading a $40, four-hour workship under the auspices of

NDCP. It begins with a slide show of "going-out parties," as Ms. Lyons calls home funerals. In the slides, families are grouped around a dead body on a bed, or in a casket or cardboard box. Ms. Lyons encourages family members to help decorate the caskets or cremation boxes, and many of them do. Caskets and cardboard boxes are lined with satin, painted like race cars or filled to overflowing with flowers.

After lunch, Ms. Lyons gets to the nitty gritty, explaining that you wash a dead body just as you would wash any bedridden person: with a soapy sponge. After washing, some people like to anoint their dead with scented oils, such as lavender or rose oil, she says, but this is purely an aesthetic preference. The proper use of dry ice—wrapped in brown paper and towels so it doesn't create a cloud of mist—will preserve a body for days. At times, the conversation becomes macabre. One participant, Sandra Waterman, is considering starting a small home-funeral business. But she doesn't own a van and wonders aloud whether her family car is big enough to transport dead bodies. Ms. Lyons says a van is preferable.

Ms. Lyons says it is legal to keep a body at home, in California, but in other states, laws about funerals, embalming (not required in most states) and keeping and transporting dead people vary considerably. A death certificate, signed by a doctor, is required almost universally.

## Zen Hospice

Diana Nichols, who calls herself "an exceedingly rational person," wouldn't have taken seriously the idea of a quality death until four years ago. Six months after he was diagnosed with liver cancer, her husband, Robert, checked into the Zen Hospice, the Victorian house where Mr. Ostaseski puts many of his Buddhist ideas about death into practice. Psychologically battered from a "dreadful" hospital stay, Ms. Nichols says her husband relaxed the minute he came through the door.

The rooms were quiet and ambient, and the volunteers, trained in meditation and Buddhist precepts such as, "Welcome everything, push nothing away," conveyed a healing calm and fearlessness, Ms. Nichols says. "It isn't tangible," she adds. "But when my husband died, he was whole again."

Mr. Nichols died peacefully one morning, two weeks after he arrived, and the volunteers suggested Ms. Nichols create an altar on his nightstand. There she put flowers from his garden, his eyeglasses, and a poem he wrote. First, she and her daughter Robin washed his body. Then they prayed together at his bedside. "It was a beautiful, beautiful death," says Ms. Nichols, who is 68. And that has helped her move through her grief. "The way he died enabled us to celebrate his life," she says.

> "*Services [for end-of-life care] . . . are underused—in large part because in our death-denying culture, many Americans don't want to discuss death and dying.*"

# Americans Are Ill Informed About How to Obtain Quality End-of-Life Care

Last Acts

Last Acts is a national coalition of organizations engaged in an education campaign to improve care for people who are dying and their families. In the following viewpoint Last Acts asserts that the majority of Americans have no control over the way they die. Unfortunately, Last Acts claims, most Americans die in pain in hospitals, away from loved ones. Last Acts recommends that Americans actively learn about end-of-life issues in order to improve their death experience.

As you read, consider the following questions:
1. What did the 1995 SUPPORT project reveal, according to Last Acts?
2. According to Last Acts, why is it becoming more urgent every day to figure out how best to care for the dying?
3. Why does Last Acts believe that the United States is at a crossroads?

During the past century, we in the United States have seen significant changes in the way we experience illness and death. A hundred years ago, people usually died from an injury or sudden illness. Farm work, factory work—even childbirth—were risky. Today, with medical and other advances, people live longer and can expect to live several years with an illness that may eventually kill them. Ultimately, many will reach a point where medical technology may be able to keep them alive but can neither restore their health nor even improve their condition. In truth, more treatment may be merely prolonging dying. At that point, patients and families face difficult choices about the kind of care they want.

## A Death-Denying Culture

While opinion polls reveal that most Americans would prefer to die at home, free from pain and with their loved ones, the reality is vastly different. Americans often die alone in hospitals or nursing homes, in pain and attached to life support machines they may not want. And this happens despite modern medicine's ability to ease most pain, the existence of good models of delivering supportive care, and the increasing availability of excellent end-of-life care through hospice and palliative care programs. All these services, however, are underused—in large part because in our death-denying culture, many Americans don't want to discuss death and dying, or because many Americans don't know about these options for good end-of-life care and thus don't ask for them.

## Beginning to Think About Dying

The last decade saw an evolution in the way Americans think about death and dying. The debate over physician-assisted suicide, coupled with pioneering studies about patterns of end-of-life care, launched a national dialogue about how we die. In November 1995, the *Journal of the American Medical Association* published initial results from SUPPORT (Study to Understand Prognoses and Preferences for Outcomes and Risks of Treatments), the largest, most widely publicized research project examining end-of-life care in the United States to date. SUPPORT documented what the public had suspected: Dying in America was unnecessarily painful and isolating, physicians did not understand patients' wishes, and it was costly. In 1997, an Institute of Medicine report, *Approaching Death in America: Improving Care at the End of Life*, underscored that "people have come to both fear a technologically over-treated and protracted death and dread the prospect of abandonment and untreated physical and emotional stress."

On the heels of SUPPORT, The Robert Wood Johnson Foundation launched Last Acts, a multiyear, multimillion-dollar national campaign to promote improvements in care and caring near the end of life. Since 1996, Last Acts has been communicating with policymakers, groups representing health care professionals, and consumer organizations about the need to make sure that seriously ill and dying patients receive the best care possible and have the fullest possible understanding of the kinds of care available.

The need for serious efforts to figure out how best to care for dying people and their loved ones is becoming more urgent every day. A large aging population, increases in the incidence of chronic disease, and the reduced availability of paid and unpaid caregivers, among other factors, must soon focus more attention on ways to improve the care we offer individuals nearing the end of their lives. . . .

Experts—and the public—generally agree that the best end-of-life care treats the whole person—body, mind and spirit. This is called *palliative care*. Palliative care works aggressively to relieve pain and other physical symptoms; it also offers emotional and spiritual support to the patient and family, while respecting their culture and traditions. Care for people near the end of life is largely financed and delivered through Medicare and Medicaid—programs that were not designed to provide comprehensive palliative care. . . .

## Public Discussion Is Necessary

Despite many recent improvements in end-of-life care and greater public awareness about it, this report shows that Americans at best have no better than a fair chance of finding good care for their loved ones or for themselves when facing a life-threatening illness. In most states, too few patients are accessing hospice and palliative care services, there are too few professionals trained in pain management and palliative care, and there are too many patients dying in hospitals and nursing homes—in pain—rather than at home with their families. . . .

We hope that this report will stimulate efforts to improve the availability and quality of the data needed to understand end-of-life care in this country, but meanwhile we hope to spark a public discussion that cannot wait until more refined data are developed.

---

## Losing Touch with Death

In the late 19th and early 20th centuries . . . the average person knew much more about death than Americans do today. It was common then for people to breathe their last at home. Children saw grandparents, parents and siblings die.

With subsequent advances in technology, doctors found ways to prolong life and researchers increasingly promised and produced cures never dreamed possible. Death increasingly occurred behind screens in hospitals. Life's ending became for most Americans a mysterious, remote, unseen and dreadful phenomenon.

August Gribbin, *Insight on the News*, February 26, 2001.

---

In a country where so much research is conducted it is remarkable that this should be the first attempt to offer a comprehensive report on a situation that ought to interest every single American. Its importance is as obvious as its urgency. Our elderly population is increasing, and as our family members and friends grow ill and die, the experience becomes vivid to every one of us. What do we know about death in this country? What are our expectations for our own care at the end of our lives? Or would we rather not think about it?

*Last Acts* offers this report to help every interested American start to understand how disturbing the current situation is and at the same time, what the elements of good end-of-life care are. It is a reminder that thinking ahead about the kind of care we want for ourselves and our families, and where we might turn to find it, is critical in averting crises when an incurable illness strikes. Thinking ahead is essential in making the end of life as peaceful as possible. . . .

# Recommendations for Action

As the data in this report indicate, Americans' likelihood of receiving good end-of-life care varies widely, depending on where they live, what they know about quality end-of-life care services and the type of care they choose. Even though some aspects of care may be better in some states than in others, in general, care for dying Americans is no better than mediocre. This is true despite years of research, improved professional education and training, the excellent record of hospice, innovation among hospitals and some nursing homes, grassroots advocacy and millions of dollars of private philanthropy—all directed at advancing the understanding and availability of good palliative care near the end of life.

*Last Acts* believes that the United States is at a crossroads. The state-by-state data we have gathered and analyzed here depict a nation that is coping poorly with critically ill and dying people *right now*. As we noted, there were no available data on spiritual and cultural issues at the end of life that could be tracked by state; however, there is no reason to believe that these matters are being well addressed nationwide. Meanwhile, demographers forecast a constantly growing number of elderly people and ever higher burdens of chronic illnesses. Much more must be done to make dying a more compassionate and caring experience, both for the patient and for the family, in America.

*Last Acts* recommends the essential steps that follow. . . .

## Actions for Everyone

1. Learn what constitutes good end-of-life care.
2. Don't be afraid to insist that your loved one, friend or neighbor receive it.
3. Join others in your state or community who are trying to make positive changes.
4. Ask your employer to have policies in place to help seriously ill employees, those caring for a seriously ill family member, and those who are bereaved.
5. Complete your own advance directive and discuss it with your family, health care proxy and physician. Update it every five years or when your health changes.
6. Encourage your spiritual leader to help your congrega-

tion explore the spiritual aspects of illness and death, and organize to help seriously ill members and their families.

7. Learn practical ways to help friends and family who are grieving.

## Americans Cannot Afford Denial

Americans have successfully avoided the unpleasant topic of death and dying for two or three generations. But now, as we begin to experience a rapid increase in the number of elderly citizens, our denial comes at a price we cannot afford—the risk of leaving more and more Americans without good, supportive, affordable care as their lives come to a close. . . .

We ardently wish that [this report] will inspire better, more thorough and complete documentation of progress at the national, state and local levels. The many people who aided *Last Acts* in compiling this report share the hope that it will raise public awareness, spur both the expectation and demand for good end-of-life care, and help everyone who cares about our future to make a clear and factual case for reform.

*"People [can] end up with decisions about their medical care that are not what they would have wanted. For that reason, it's important to plan in advance for your end-of-life care."*

# Advance Directives Are Improving End-of-Life Care

*Tufts University Health & Nutrition Letter*

When a terminally ill patient cannot speak for himself or herself about what end-of-life treatment is desired, the result is often disagreements over what should be done, and medical treatment that the patient may not have wanted. The following viewpoint from the *Tufts University Health & Nutrition Letter* advocates advance directives as a way of avoiding such conflict. According to the viewpoint, through these legally binding documents—that specify what happens when someone is too ill to speak for himself or herself—people can ensure that their end-of-life wishes are honored. The monthly *Tufts University Health & Nutrition Letter* is dedicated to providing scientifically authoritative health and nutrition advice.

As you read, consider the following questions:

1. Why was Nancy Cruzan's case taken all the way to the Supreme Court, according to the author?
2. According to Linda Emanuel, what is a common myth about living wills?
3. Why is a health care proxy necessary in addition to a living will, in the author's opinion?

*Tufts University Health & Nutrition Letter,* "Making End-of-Life Medical Decisions Ahead of Time," vol. 20, September 2002, p. 4. Copyright © 2002 by *Tufts University Health & Nutrition Letter.* Reproduced by permission of the Copyright Clearance Center, Inc.

In 1983, a 26-year-old Missouri woman named Nancy Cruzan was rendered permanently unconscious in a car accident. Her heart was beating and she could breathe on her own, but she depended on a feeding tube to survive. After Ms. Cruzan had spent 5 years in that condition—medically termed a "persistent vegetative state"—her family asked for the feeding tube to be removed. Hospital personnel refused, and the case went through years of legal wrangling, all the way up to the Supreme Court.

In 1990, an 86-year-old Minnesota woman named Helga Wanglie developed respiratory failure 2 weeks after breaking a hip. She was put on a respirator to help her breathe, but doctors were then unable to wean her from the machine. Several months later, Mrs. Wanglie's heart and lungs stopped; she was resuscitated but left unconscious and severely brain-damaged. She was then given a feeding tube; however, her doctors felt that her prognosis was so poor that sustaining her through artificial means was futile and medically inappropriate. Her family disagreed, saying that Mrs. Wanglie believed in the intrinsic value of life. Again, it was left to the court system to decide the outcome.

The reason such personal choices ended up in being made by strangers in a courtroom is that neither Ms. Cruzan nor Mrs. Wanglie had completed a living will, a document that would have outlined their feelings about accepting or refusing life-sustaining treatment in the face of severe disability. Nor had they signed a health-care proxy, a document that authorizes a trusted person to make medical decisions on one's behalf.

Living wills and health care proxies are types of "advance directives"—legally binding documents that translate your wishes about what happens to you when you're too ill to speak for yourself. Most people, understandably, don't fill them out. Illness and death are difficult to contemplate, much less discuss with loved ones. But not everyone dies peacefully in his or her sleep after reaching old age. The upshot: Family disagreements on the direction of care, or state interests like a legal obligation to preserve life, can mean that people end up with decisions about their medical care that are not what they would have wanted. For that reason, it's important to plan in advance for your end-of-life care while you're still well.

## Living Will: Before You Dot the "i's"

Simply put, a living will records in writing whether or not you'd want certain medical treatments that might be needed to sustain your life. It also serves as a guide to your values and preferences in medical care, telling family and health-care providers, for instance, whether you want to live as long as possible or let death come as it may.

A common myth about living wills, says Linda Emanuel, MD, PhD, an ethicist and professor of medicine at Northwestern Medical School [in Chicago], is that they're "all about resuscitation"—in other words, simply for letting doctors know whether or not you want cardiopulmonary resuscitation (CPR) if your heart stops. But a living will can also record your preferences for a number of life-sustaining treatments in addition to CPR, such as ventilation (artificial breathing), feeding tubes, major surgery, blood transfusions, or antibiotics to treat life-threatening infections like pneumonia.

Another myth, says Dr. Emanuel, is that "an advance-care document is necessarily about avoiding unwanted aggressive intervention"—in other words, all about "pulling the plug." In actuality, she says, "a well-designed document will allow for a range of opinions and preferences in care if you're seriously ill." For instance, you may wish to specify treatments that you do want, such as pain management, or nursing care at home rather than in the hospital. You might also make clear that you want doctors to employ whatever measures they can to help you get better while you hold out hope for recovery. Not everyone opts to "shut off the machine."

You don't need a lawyer to draw up a living will. In fact, the professional you'll want to speak with early in the process should be your doctor. Unfortunately, the reluctance that stalls laypeople from talking about end-of-life issues extends to physicians, too, who may feel squeamish about bringing up the subject with their patients. "Patients many need to take the initiative to address the subject first," says David Doukas, MD, a senior fellow at the Center for Bioethics and associate professor of family medicine at the

University of Pennsylvania School of Medicine.

Having such a conversation could prove well worth any initial discomfort. For example, you may feel strongly that you don't ever want to be "hooked up to tubes" in the event of an accident or serious illness. But that general phrase can mean many different things in terms of specific medical treatments. Consider that while you might think of an artificial breathing tube as an "extreme measure" and prefer that it not be used to sustain your life over the long term, you may opt for a tube to administer antibiotics directly into your blood vessels, if needed. Your doctor will be able to help ground you in the basics of these and other treatments generally covered in a living will.

---

## Few Americans Have Advance Directives

Although advance directive policies are determined primarily at the state level, in 1991, Congress enacted the Patient Self-Determination Act (PSDA). This act requires that all health care facilities receiving Medicare or Medicaid reimbursements must inform patients of their right to make choices about the treatment they receive and to prepare advance directives. . . .

Despite the PSDA's requirement that health care providers tell patients about advance directives, surprisingly few Americans actually complete these documents. A study published in 2002 estimated the overall prevalence of advance directives to be 15 to 20 percent in the general population. Rates of completion are also low in the populations that most need them. A 2002 study of nursing home residents found that only 20 percent of them had living wills, and 48 percent had DNR [do not resuscitate] orders.

Last Acts, "Means to a Better End: A Report on Dying in America Today," November 2002.

---

Before writing up the document, spend some time thinking through exactly what you want, talking with family, friends, and clergy to better define your values and preferences. Do you want to live as long as possible, whatever the quality of life? Or would you rather just be made comfortable? Do your answers depend on your prognosis? (A 5 percent chance means different things to different people.) Any document that goes into effect without discussion is likely to have consequences that do not truly reflect the patient's wishes in end-of-life care, says Northwestern's Dr. Emanuel.

## The Legalese

Whatever is specified in a living will, the document itself must comply with state law—a highly confusing patchwork of regulations that differs from state to state. To get your state's rules and forms, contact your state attorney general's office, representative's office, or medical association. Partnership For Caring . . . also makes state-specific forms available. And the American Bar Association's Commission on Legal Problems of the Elderly . . . offers a general form covering most state requirements on its website.

For those turned off by legalese, the Florida-based organization Aging With Dignity . . . offers a combined living will and health-care proxy called "Five Wishes," which uses friendlier language and includes sections on how you'd like to be cared for and how you'd like to be remembered by loved ones. It's valid in 35 states.

## Assigning a Health-Care Proxy

No matter how detailed, no living will can anticipate all possible situations. For instance, perhaps yours covers CPR and tube feeding but not antibiotic treatment—and you develop a life-threatening infection while in the hospital. That's where a document called a health-care proxy or medical power of attorney comes in. This document names, and legally authorizes, a trusted person to direct your medical care if you can't do so yourself.

Some states have hierarchies that specify who is allowed to make decisions for a person who's incapacitated in cases where no health-care proxy has been named. In Illinois, for example, priority goes from a patient's legal guardian to his or her spouse, adult sons or daughters, parents, adult brothers or sisters, adult grandchildren, a close friend, and guardian of the estate—in that order. But that can create conflict if, say, your spouse from a second marriage is authorized to make decisions but your adult children from the first marriage want to participate as well. Then, too, there may sometimes be a few family members with equal votes who must agree as a group, such as siblings or adult children.

Thinking about who to name as your health-care proxy should begin early in the advance-care planning process. Once you do choose one, Dr. Emanuel suggests working through different scenarios to determine your personal threshold for medical care. Say you have Alzheimer's disease. If you reach the point where you can't be left alone, will your proxy decide to admit you to a long-term care facility or arrange for round-the-clock care in your home?

Working through such questions with your proxy—even handing over your pencil for him or her to fill in the blanks—can serve as a kind of rehearsal. "It's symbolic," says Dr. Emanuel. "It reduces the burden for your proxy, the regret of having to make a decision, and it helps them understand they're just being the patient's agent."

Once you have your signed papers in hand—both the health-care proxy and living will—don't stash them away in a safe-deposit box, where they might not be easily available if needed. Tragically, some people's wishes haven't been followed simply because the papers couldn't be found.

*"Though 'advance directives' . . . are at least in theory legally binding—in reality, they have their limitations. Sometimes they simply are not followed."*

# Advance Directives Do Not Always Improve End-of-Life Care

Valerie Reitman

Advance directives are legally binding documents that specify what medical treatments should take place in the event that a person is too ill to speak for himself or herself. While these documents can be very helpful in making end-of-life decisions, they do not automatically prevent all conflicts, argues Valerie Reitman in the following viewpoint. She points out that doctors' first priority is usually to preserve life despite the existence of an advance directive specifying otherwise. In addition, she says, most directives are not specific enough to anticipate all circumstances and often result in disagreement about what end-of-life decisions to make. Reitman is a staff writer for the *Los Angeles Times*.

As you read, consider the following questions:
1. According to Reitman, what event has prompted thousands of Americans to request advance directives?
2. In the author's opinion, why does the development of new technology mean that advance directives are not always followed?
3. What percentage of Americans have written advance directives, according to the author?

W hen death seemed near at age 82, Foster Lockhart was more prepared than most people. The retired police officer and his family had talked over how he wanted to die, and he had written his wishes down in a properly witnessed document.

He had specified that his wife would make any healthcare decisions if he wasn't able and that no life-support measures were to be taken if he were unconscious or there was no chance of recovery. He particularly noted that he did not want to have dialysis started under any conditions.

But three years ago [in 2000] when he was admitted to a Phoenix-area hospital with fluid filling his lungs, his blood pressure plummeting and a large aneurysm threatening to erupt, his wishes were ignored, says his daughter, Carol Lockhart. The hospital started preparing him for dialysis at the behest of his doctor.

## Many Limitations

Though "advance directives" such as Foster Lockhart's are at least in theory legally binding—in reality, they have their limitations. Sometimes they simply are not followed. Family members may disagree with them or with one another, leading to lengthy legal delays. The documents cannot usually specify the moment when "enough is enough." And patients and their families also have to fight physicians' efforts to keep the patient alive.

In the last few weeks [November 2003], thousands of Americans have requested the directives, also known as "living wills," which outline how patients want to be treated in the event they can't communicate their wishes. The interest has been prompted, say agencies offering the forms, by the Terri Schiavo case in Florida—in which the state Legislature and Gov. Jeb Bush have intervened to continue life support for a 39-year-old woman who has been in a vegetative state for 13 years.

Having such a document can certainly help eliminate confusion about the patient's desires and often can spare family members guilt. Had Schiavo written down her wishes and had them properly witnessed, it would undoubtedly have made it easier to terminate life-support systems—as her husband claims his wife said she wanted—because most courts will honor the patient's wishes. (A state court had agreed to stop life support before the Legislature and governor intervened; Schiavo's parents want it continued.)[1]

But a directive doesn't automatically prevent all problems.

When Carol Lockhart asked if her father could possibly survive even with the dialysis, the doctors said he could not. "He's going to die anyway," she remembers pleading with hospital doctors as she and her mother urged them to honor her father's wishes.

Only after she brought in a hospice physician to plead the case did the hospital staff finally cease the treatments.

"Advance directives are funny things," says Dr. Neil Wenger, a medical professor at UCLA [University of California, Los Angeles] and director of its new Healthcare Ethics Center. "You can fill one out and it wouldn't guide much," he says.

Unless the document directly specifies a surrogate to make the health-care decisions on behalf of the patient—or describes the exact health situation, which is difficult to predict, "it's unlikely to go too far in alleviating a controversy," Wenger says.

## Key Documents

Requirements for advance directives vary by state. Generally, two documents are called for: a living will, or instructions describing the treatment one would want if too sick to communicate; and the designation of a "durable power of attorney for health care," to make decisions on your behalf. In California, they are combined in a single document called an "Advance Health Care Directive."

The living will can be simple, reflecting the quality of life the patient would want to maintain, or specific, outlining what he or she would want in various scenarios—from forbidding electroshock therapy in case of admission to a psychiatric hospital to differentiating between a coma and a

---

1. After Schiavo's husband won a court case to have her feeding tubes removed, Florida governor Jeb Bush passed a law giving him executive authority over her care instead and ordered the tube be reinserted. In 2004 this law was ruled unconstitutional. As of this writing, the legal battle over Shiavo continued, with her parents attempting to keep her alive and her husband arguing for removal of the tube.

vegetative state. The patient can also specify that he or she wants to be kept alive by all available means.

Also available are "do-not-resuscitate orders" in the event of cardiac arrest. They must be signed by a physician and tend to be used only if the person has a terminal condition.

One reason advance directives aren't always followed is that technology can now keep patients alive in situations that usually cannot be anticipated—or described—by the layperson.

"Most people are not well enough informed to know what they might need, particularly younger, healthier people," says Barbara E. Volk-Craft, co-director of Healthcare Decisions, part of a Phoenix-based hospice program that educates people and institutions about the directive.

## Difficulty of Creating a Living Will

People must . . . grapple with drafting complex instructions. Studies find that living wills regularly contain mutually inconsistent instructions. Nor do the standard forms sufficiently help. One version deploys vague terms like "artificial means" and "heroic measures." Another asks the writer to specify numerous treatments for numerous conditions, a labor of analysis few of us are equipped to undertake.

Angela Fagerlin and Carl E. Schneider, *Los Angeles Times*, November 12, 2003.

Typical "advance directive" documents describe general scenarios and leave room for patients to indicate any specifics. For instance, a common one known as "Five Wishes" says if "my doctor and another healthcare professional both decide that I am likely to die within a short period of time, and life-support treatment would only delay the moment of my death," (choose one): "I want to have life-support treatment, I don't want life-support treatment. If it has been started, I want it stopped," or "I want to have life-support treatment if my doctor believes it could help. But I want my doctor to stop giving me life-support treatment if it is not helping my health condition or symptoms."

But when a patient is rushed to the hospital, the first priority for the medical staff is to keep the patient alive.

"When you get caught in high-tech lifesaving, aggressive management of treatment," says Volk-Craft, "it's hard to stop that train."

Nearly every day, emergency room workers face some dilemma about resuscitation—either what they think is the best thing or what the family wants, says Dr. Catherine Marco, an ER [emergency room] doctor in Toledo, Ohio, who also chairs the ethics committee of the American College of Emergency Physicians.

Surveys suggest a wide range in how such situations are handled across the country, she says. Few patients have directives—estimates vary from 10% to 20% of Americans—and even those who do often arrive at the hospital without them, with their loved ones not knowing where the document is.

"We found some [doctors] very lenient and will accept the family's word, while others are very strict and will attempt to resuscitate unless they have a document in hand," Marco says. "The problem is bridging the gap between what the patient wants and what we do."

Legal concerns also factor into most physicians' thinking. In a recent survey, 94% of emergency physicians said concerns that they'd be sued (if they didn't do everything possible) influenced their decision-making, even though 78% said that in a perfect world, they shouldn't.

## Finding Agreement

Some families deliberate for days even when they have the patient's directive in hand, medical officials say. "There's a tremendous amount of stress if everybody doesn't agree," says the Rev. Karyn Reddick, director of pastoral care at Long Beach Memorial Medical Center. In those cases, clergy, medical staff and family will discuss the matter together. "It takes a lot of time to work through the issues and come to a place" where the entire family can live with the decision.

While most people designate a spouse, parent or adult child as the surrogate decision maker, sometimes the designee will not know the patient's wishes or even that he or she has been entrusted with making the decisions.

Particularly problematic are the cases in which the person leaves the decision up to someone other than a spouse or children, says Wenger, of UCLA's ethics center. In these cases, it's important that the person explain his choice to his doctor and family when he fills out the advance directive.

"Think of the problems when it comes out that the golfing partner gets to decide, and the spouse and children are left to wonder why they weren't chosen," Wenger says. "The goal is to alleviate controversy."

In cases where there is no directive, most states specify a hierarchy—with an unestranged spouse usually given such decision-making power, followed by an adult child or parent.

For example, a woman treated at UCLA for a brain disease had an advance directive specifying that the husband was to make decisions on her behalf, and that her estranged sisters in another country were not to be contacted.

Before they had seen the advance directive, the hospital contacted the sisters. When the rest of the family arrived, they wanted everything done, although the husband insisted she wouldn't want that.

But when family members were shown the advance directive with the patient's wishes clearly listed, they stopped protesting. "Simply circulating that advance directive to her family was very useful," Wenger says. "If it's not clear who your surrogate would be, or your family is likely to argue or they wouldn't know your preferences, an advance directive is a wonderful way of indicating it."

Without a directive stating otherwise, a gay or cohabiting partner would legally not have any influence in most states, says John Mayoue, a family-law attorney in Atlanta, who notes that 5 million people in the last census [2000] were in such relationships. He urges people to reinforce their written wishes with a video of themselves that can be played for family members.

## Easing Guilt

Still, having a document can ease any lingering guilt for the surrogate, who often is their spouse or closest relative and might have the most difficulty deciding to end the person's life because they will be the most bereft.

Not long after being diagnosed with ovarian cancer four years ago [1999], Nellie Ortega insisted that her husband, Ruben, sit down with her to discuss the care she wanted. She wrote an advance directive and designated her husband as decision-maker.

She was hospitalized several times for treatments that failed to halt her cancer. Last year [2002], she decided enough was enough. She told her husband that she did not want to be resuscitated and that she wanted her feeding tube removed.

Two days later, Ruben summoned paramedics when Nellie started having difficulty breathing. They gave her oxygen and suggested bringing her to the hospital. "My first wish was to keep her alive at all costs," says Ruben, who lives in Glendale, Ariz. "But then I remembered what she wanted. I brought out the advance directive."

She slipped into a coma and died in a few hours.

"As difficult as it was, it was made easier by the fact that I was doing what she wanted me to."

> *"The goals of hospice . . . are to meet all of a person's needs—not just medical ones. . . . The services are tailored to each patient and family."*

# Hospice Care Is Benefiting the Terminally Ill

Part I: Jack D. Gordon; Part II: Stephen Kiernan

The authors of the following two-part viewpoint contend that many terminally ill people are benefitting from hospice care. In Part I Jack D. Gordon, president of the Hospice Foundation of America, maintains that hospice care is improving the death experience for a large number of the terminally ill and their families. In Part II *Burlington Free Press* staff writer Stephen Kiernan describes the benefits of hospice care, as experienced by Arthur Goyette and his terminally ill wife Betty. Hospice workers focus on providing a high quality of life for the dying, explains Kiernan, with an emphasis on physical comfort and spiritual care.

As you read, consider the following questions:

1. According to Gordon, how many Americans took advantage of hospice care in 2003?
2. Why did Arthur Goyette become ill, as cited by Kiernan?
3. What is the average daily cost of hospice care compared to hospital care, as cited by the author?

# I

On the day we are born, we are surrounded by love, with many people committed to bringing us through the birth process as gently as possible.

But the day we die is too often a merciful deliverance from an extended period of discomfort and pain, imposed by an uncaring, institutionalized medical system.

Rather than being a release from suffering, dying should be more of a gentle transition through one of life's natural processes, eased by compassionate care and the presence and support of loved ones.

Fortunately, there is a medical system that delivers that care. It is called hospice, and last year [2003] almost one-half million Americans took advantage of this special kind of caring.

In hospice, pain and discomfort are controlled. The unit of care is the family as well as the patient, and an array of services is offered to ease the emotional, psychological and spiritual stress that comes with a loved one's death. The family receives ongoing support even after the patient dies.

Hospice is most often appropriate when a patient is in the last few months of a terminal illness and when aggressive therapies are no longer working. Isn't it better to die surrounded by love rather than being surrounded by machines?

Hospice services are covered by Medicare, Medicaid and most insurance programs, including HMOs [health maintenance organizations].

If you know of someone who is approaching the end stage of a terminal illness, it is their right to be offered the hospice option.

# II

Arthur Goyette's wife, Betty, has fought ovarian cancer since the spring of 1998. Her battle is nearly over.

"She is terminal now," Arthur said recently [in 2003].

Betty is a resident at Vermont Respite House in Williston, an inpatient facility for people with less than six months to live.

The celebration of Betty's life continues. In April [2003], the family threw a party to celebrate five years since her first diagnosis. In May, one daughter ran the Vermont City Marathon wearing a T-shirt that said, "Miles for Mom and me."

This month [September 2003], Arthur is at her bedside each day when she wakes from her mid-day nap.

Betty went through three surgeries and two rounds of chemotherapy. Before moving to the Respite House [a hospice] she had fallen, by Arthur's count, 61 times. Now she is bedridden.

Yet Arthur smiles when he reflects on the past five years.

"It has been a beautiful journey," he says, shaking his head. "Just beautiful."

Arthur and Betty are proof that a terminal illness need not be gloomy. They are proof people can die in comfort and dignity and peace if given proper end-of-life care. . . .

## A Labor of Love

Arthur Goyette, a Burlington native, met Betty Brault in the early 1950s at a St. Michael's College dance. She was a nursing student from Winooski [Vermont].

They married in 1958 and had five children. For 42 years, they have lived on Caroline Street.

Arthur worked for the family wholesale business. Betty raised the children and sang in the choir at Christ the King Church. She is 66 and he is 68.

Most of their lives they enjoyed good health, and almost every evening they took an hour's walk through the neighborhood. Friends often saw them come home holding hands.

In April 1998, doctors found that Betty had an ovarian tumor. "The operation to take it out was supposed to take three hours," Arthur recalled. "It turned out 7."

The tumor weighed 10 pounds, he said. Betty underwent chemotherapy and radiation. The cancer seemed to be gone, Arthur said, although fear of a relapse "always sits on your shoulder."

Three years later, Betty had a tumor in her brain.

"Ovarian to brain is very unusual," Arthur said.

Betty had surgery right away. She lost some short-term memory, he said, and her balance was unsteady. Healing was difficult; so was taking care of her.

Ten months later, another brain tumor appeared.

"It was the same cancer, in the same place," Arthur recalled. "Again she elected to have the surgery. I couldn't believe she'd do it a second time.

"It's all a question of will to live and trust in the doctor."

That surgery also involved a protracted recovery.

"I called it a 36-hours-a-day job," Arthur said. He shrugged. "Hey, the washer's in the cellar, the bedroom's upstairs."

Then, in April 2002, one of Betty's eyes began to close. "The eye had almost totally shut," he said, "and she had trouble turning her head."

She had a tumor in her neck.

When doctors offered Betty a chance to participate in a trial of a new chemotherapy, "she immediately said 'yes,'" Arthur said. "They said, 'Whoa. You need to meet with the people, the doctors, and hear what it's about.'"

She soon accepted the treatment.

"In two weeks the eye started opening up," Arthur said. "It wasn't long after that you couldn't even feel the tumor in her neck anymore."

Caring for his wife during this recovery became more difficult.

"She was in a wheelchair, and I didn't want to strap her in," he said. "But you need to do the dishes, or the phone rings and you turn your head for a second. Then she'd see a bit of dust, and reach for it without thinking, and bang, down.

"She fell 61 times."

Arthur frowned. "I ended up using the belt, bed rails, monitors."

Those compromises were insufficient, Arthur said, because Betty needed constant care.

"Three major operations and then chemo, it knocks you down," he said. "You can't kill all those cells without other effects."

When she became incontinent, he began getting up with her every two hours at night.

"It was a labor of love," he said. "I'd do it again in a heartbeat."

## A Second Patient

The care-giving took its toll; Arthur became sick.

"Pneumonia," he said. "I had stopped taking care of myself, and it caught up with me." That was followed by a bout of bronchitis.

"It's not that we hadn't had help," Arthur said. "My kids were great, but they can only do so much. We had tons of neighbors' help, meals cooked and so forth. But I was so maxed out at that point."

Neighbors rallied. One began taking the family's garbage to the dump. When another neighbor visited to drop off a meal, Arthur happened to mention that Betty had never ridden in a convertible.

---

### Principles of Hospice Care

Hospice is a philosophy of care. The hospice philosophy recognizes death as the final stage of life and seeks to enable patients to continue an alert, pain-free life and to manage other symptoms so that their last days may be spent with dignity and quality, surrounded by their loved ones. Hospice affirms life and neither hastens nor postpones death. Hospice care treats the person rather than the disease; it emphasizes quality rather than length of life. It provides family-centered care involving the patient and family in making decisions. Care is provided for the patient and family 24 hours-a-day and 7 days-a-week. Hospice care can be given in the patient's home, a hospital, nursing home, or private hospice facility.

American Cancer Society, 2004.

---

"A few days later the doorbell rings, and there's a Chrysler Sebring convertible, brand new, like about 6,000 miles on it," he said. "It wasn't perfect weather, but we had a great ride. Betty was in there like a queen, neighbors taking pictures. We went and got the grandkids and took them for a creemee [ice cream].

"Two days later the woman rings again. She says the weather wasn't so great last time, and here's another Sebring."

Despite the help and happier times, Arthur couldn't keep up.

"It was too much, and I resisted getting help. . . . But I couldn't do a thing, write a check or anything. So I'd get up early in the morning, turn on the monitor and get busy. When she woke up I'd run up the stairs."

A friend told his daughter about Visiting Nurse Association's [VNA] hospice program, which provides support at home for patients and their families.

Arthur remained reluctant. "I wasn't going to do that. I was going to do it all."

Eventually fatigue won out. He asked his daughter to make the call to the VNA, but soon he was on the line, too.

"I was . . . on the phone, and the woman was telling us that we were definitely eligible," he said. "One thing I'll never forget: The woman's name was Angel."

## All the Needs

Angel Collins is associate director of the VNA's Hospice of the Champlain Valley [Vermont].

The goals of hospice, she says, are to meet all of a person's needs—not just medical ones—and to enable people to die at home if they wish. The services are tailored to each patient and family, she said.

Hospice is less expensive than hospital care. One day in an intensive care unit can cost $2,000; hospice typically runs $120 per day.

In Betty's case, her needs evolved. First, a VNA nurse came to provide medical care. Then an aide visited three times a week to give her a bath. Social workers came periodically to help the family handle emotional issues. Later, volunteers began helping around the house, keeping Betty company and giving Arthur an occasional break.

The VNA has 225 hospice volunteers, Collins said. "It is a fundamental component of the hospice mission to involve the community."

The volunteers, Arthur says, "still visit Betty now, every one of them. . . . They sent all of these caring, loving people to us. I can't even put it into words."

## A Final Home

As Betty struggled to recover, she began to make decisions.

"After the second brain surgery, she said no more operations," Arthur said. "After the second chemo, she said enough of that. . . . I felt it was her decision to make, and I would honor it."

The cancer was not gone, Arthur said, but they did not

pursue tests to track its spread.

"Why spend $600 for a CAT scan when she doesn't want any more surgery or chemo?" he said.

For Betty and Arthur, the next step was a move to the Vermont Respite House. The 14-bed facility in Williston applies the hospice approach to inpatient residents. Hospice staff provide care, aided by 120 additional volunteers, administrator Sharon Keegan said.

"When the realization comes that nothing more can really be done," Keegan said, "the question is how do you live the best you can with the remaining days that you have?

"It's as different as [Ludwig van] Beethoven and Joe Cocker," she said. Fans of either musician might be offended by spending their last days hearing the other. "What music do you want to die to?"

The musical choice exemplifies a whole range of options at the end of life, Keegan said.

"In the final journey, a lot of priorities become more available. Our work is being able to listen fully to what someone is asking, and to make that care come about."

The Respite House extends its respect for patients beyond their deaths, Keegan said. When a patient dies, the room is kept empty for several days.

"We want to allow the family time to come back and feel whatever they feel by returning here," she said. "And we want the staff to have time to process the loss, as well."

The Respite House, from Arthur's perspective, was the perfect move.

"It's a home," he said. "They treat people as individuals. One day my wife slept till 10:45, and the person said, 'You don't want breakfast, Betty. You want brunch.'"

He said the setting was comfortable, with gardens and a bird feeder outside each room. More importantly, he said, the staff performed beyond his expectations.

"They're all there because they want to be," Arthur said, "It's not because they're overpaid. It's a love of what they're doing. It is so obvious, the tender loving care that pours out of them."

On his birthday, June 24, Arthur brought Betty the cards he'd received, so she could open them and share in the day.

But she was confused, and didn't understand.

"I guess they could tell I was feeling low about that," he said, "because at lunch all the Respite House folks came out banging pots and pans and singing me Happy Birthday. . . . That place is just so special."

Betty now has a daily routine.

Hospice volunteers spend the morning with her, while Arthur takes care of the house and himself. When Communion is available, she receives it. She takes a nap into the afternoon. And when she awakes, Arthur is there.

"Every day," he said. "For as long as it takes."

## Preparing to Go

Arthur tries not to think about what will happen next.

"I don't have any control over what happens, and neither does she. . . . Who knows, with the way she fights?"

Betty has begun having discomfort in her arms, he said. "They're controlling it with morphine and whatnot."

Arthur has to remember his own pain, too, he said. He attends a caregivers' support group. He is reading books like "Final Gifts" by Maggie Callanan and "Men and Grief" by Carol Staudacher.

When the topic of assisted suicide comes up, Arthur gives an emphatic thumbs-down. He says he would never trade the experience he and Betty shared in the past five years.

"We'd have missed our 40th wedding anniversary," he said. "We were there for the birth of our daughter's second child. We've had all different memories and occasions. And we still have them, even now."

Arthur sat forward and pressed his palms together. "I am so glad that she has fought as hard as she has. She has been an example to so many people. Her faith is strong for people, too, certainly to my kids.

"She is at peace now," Arthur said. "She told me two nights ago that she wants to live, she's got too much going on, family and all. . . .

"But she's ready. She's at peace."

Arthur said he has reconciled himself, too.

"I'm ready to let her go. I don't want to, but it's her battle. I have told her, 'I'll do anything you want to keep you going.' I also told her I am willing to let her go. . . .

"She's certainly had enough. . . . You have to say your goodbyes and let them know it's all OK. It's very important for them."

## Family Gathering

Arthur and Betty's five children are preparing, too. They have written Betty letters. One daughter accepted a job in California but negotiated a monthly return to Vermont. A son visited from Arizona. Her local children often go to the Respite House.

The family came together May 17 [2003] for the Respite House's annual fund-raising road race, when 300 people raised $31,000.

One of Betty's daughters ran the race, another took snapshots at the finish line, and Arthur stood behind Betty's wheelchair like a bodyguard in porkpie hat.

Betty sat calmly through it all under a wide straw hat, her hands folded in her blanketed lap.

After the race one sweaty runner leaned down and asked her, "Are you having a good day?"

She focused on him and smiled. "Every day is a good day."

"*[Among minorities there] is a very strong
reluctance to give up aggressive treatment
options at the end of life, even when
palliative care or hospice care may be more
appropriate.*"

# Many Minorities Are Not Benefiting from Hospice Care

Gwen London

Minority groups are far less likely than white Americans to
benefit from hospice care, maintains Gwen London in the
following viewpoint. There is widespread distrust of the
health care system among minorities, a reluctance to give up
hospital treatment, and a common feeling that accepting hospice care means giving up belief in God, argues London. For
these reasons, she says, terminally ill minorities often do not
utilize the benefits of end-of-life hospice care. Since 1982,
London has been an advocate for improving end-of-life care
through better palliative and hospice services.

As you read, consider the following questions:
1. In the author's opinion, why are many minorities
   unwilling to forgo aggressive treatment for terminal
   conditions?
2. Why are minorities often suspicious of pain medication,
   according to London?
3. Why do African American physicians need better
   education about palliative care, as argued by the author?

Gwen London, testimony before an APA Senate hearing, July 18, 2000.

I have been personally involved in end-of-life care since 1962 when I became a volunteer at Hospice of Washington, the first inpatient hospice facility in the country. Since that time, my work as a hospice chaplain, a hospital chaplain and as associate minister of an 1800-member urban church has provided me with many rich opportunities to minister to persons during their last days of life. From these various professional opportunities and from my own personal experience as an African-American woman in ministry, I have formed what I think is a first-hand perspective on the issues of minorities dealing with care at the end of life.

## Distrust of the Medical Establishment

I believe that lack of trust is the major factor in the way that members of minority communities interface with the healthcare system at all stages of the life spectrum and particularly at the end of life. Since my background has been primarily in working in the African-American community, I would like to start from that frame of reference but I believe that many of the factors that come into play can be extrapolated to other minority groups.

Many studies have shown that African-Americans are less likely than white Americans to receive a wide range of medical services, including potentially life-saving surgical procedures. In fact, the pattern of receiving less than optimal health care starts before birth and extends throughout the dying process. National statistics document higher infant mortality rates, inadequate preventive care, disparities in recommendations for medical treatments and higher death rates for diseases such as cardiovascular disease, cancer and AIDS. Because of this pattern of lack of access to health care as well as well-documented historical incidents of research and treatment abuse, minority patients and family members are less likely to feel that members of the medical establishment can be trusted to serve their best interests or even try to understand their feelings and concerns when a medical crisis arises. Because this attitude of suspicion and mistrust is usually unspoken, and because it is very different from the way that most physicians think that they are viewed, it becomes a barrier that is often difficult to identify and even more difficult to overcome.

## Reluctance to Accept Hospice Care

The primary result of this attitude of distrust is a very strong reluctance to give up aggressive treatment options at the end of life, even when palliative care or hospice care may be more appropriate. By aggressive treatment I mean the continued utilization of the wide range of invasive medical treatments that are geared toward cure, even when the patient's disease has clearly reached a point where cure is no longer a possibility.

Many older members of minority communities have not traditionally had access to health care. Therefore, when they are finally eligible to receive benefits under Medicare they have a very strong desire to receive everything that the healthcare system has to offer. When asked to forgo aggressive treatment for terminal conditions or when advised that hospice or palliative care may be more appropriate, they are unwilling to give up their hard earned entitlement. I have worked with patients who have been adamant in their refusal to consider admission to a hospice until they have had that one last hospitalization during which the physician indicates that there is nothing more that can be done. Because minority patients have had so little access to health care, extraordinary measures are viewed as acceptable, and many patients will express that they want everything done even if that means that they end up on life support machines, an attitude that often conflicts with the view of the health provider.

Because of the high incidence of drug addiction in many minority communities, there is a great ambivalence regarding the use of narcotics for pain relief. Many patients have first-hand experience in their families or their communities so the efforts of the health professional to encourage the use of narcotics for pain control are met with suspicion and resistance even in terminal conditions that are accompanied by a great deal of pain. I have heard patients express that there is a conspiracy in this country to control the African-American community by turning everyone into drug addicts, so other methods of pain control often have to be tried before narcotics can even be suggested, even when the stronger medication is clearly indicated.

From a financial perspective, the dying person is often the sole or primary provider of income from some form of pen-

## Hospice Care Patients

Number and percent distribution of current hospice care patients and mean and median length of service in days, by selected characteristics: United States, 2000.

| Patient characteristic | Number | Percent distribution |
|---|---|---|
| Total | 105,500 | 100.0 |
| **Age** | | |
| Under 65 years | 19,600 | 18.6 |
| Under 45 years | 4,800 | 4.5 |
| 45–64 years | 14,800 | 14.1 |
| 65 years and over | 85,900 | 81.4 |
| 65–69 years | 7,700 | 7.3 |
| 70–74 years | 10,500 | 9.9 |
| 75–79 years | 22,100 | 20.9 |
| 80–84 years | 16,900 | 16.1 |
| 85 years and over | 28,700 | 27.3 |
| **Sex** | | |
| Male | 44,900 | 42.6 |
| Female | 60,600 | 57.4 |
| **Hispanic or Latino origin** | | |
| Hispanic | 5,400 | 5.1 |
| Not-Hispanic | 83,400 | 79.1 |
| Unknown | 16,700 | 15.8 |
| **Race** | | |
| White | 87,300 | 82.8 |
| Black and other† | 13,000 | 12.3 |
| Black | 11,200 | 10.6 |
| Unknown | 5,200 | 5.0 |

† Other race includes Asian, Native Hawaiian or other Pacific Islander, American Indian or Alaska Native, and multiple races.

Centers for Disease Control and Prevention, February 2004.

sion, so the death of the patient creates a severe threat to the family's financial well-being. Therefore the patient and family focus is on extending life through all possible means rather than allowing the illness to progress along a natural course, again an unspoken concern not usually understood by health providers.

## Different Belief System

Many members of minority communities equate the acceptance of hospice or palliative treatment with giving up on

God's chance to perform a miracle or cure. Believing that only God can determine when a person will die, they are not willing to accept the fact that a family member is dying and often express their reluctance to forego aggressive treatment with the sentiment, "Where there is life, there is hope." Because a theology of suffering is often an integral part of the religion practiced by many minority groups, a physician's efforts to press for palliative care as a method of relieving pain is often seen as the physician's attempts to play God. This is interpreted as a violation of the patient's personal covenant with God, a major taboo for persons of color.

Spiritual care plays a very important part in the lives of minority patients and families. By spiritual care I mean the multiplicity of religions and faith traditions present in the minority community. Because many patients belong to spiritual communities that they or other family members have helped to establish, it is not unusual for a patient to have been a part of a specific faith group or spiritual community for more than 40 years. Because this faith perspective is central to the world view of the minority patient and family it tends to influence all considerations and decisions in the event of a health crisis. This is particularly true at the end of life. In the absence of the possibility of a medical cure, the patient is forced to fall back on their belief in a God who is all-knowing and all-powerful, and this belief takes precedence over the rational logic that is usually applied by the members of the medical establishment. Again, the inherent distrust makes it difficult if not impossible to rely on a physician when the physician's view is diametrically opposed to the faith of the patient and family beliefs.

## Improving End-of-Life Care for Minorities

A number of things can be done to better address the concerns of minority communities relating to end-of-life care in the future. First, we need to develop a comprehensive physician education effort to sensitize physicians and other members of the healthcare system to the pervasive impact of the unspoken attitude of distrust that is an integral part of minority perceptions about health care, particularly as it relates to care at the end of life. At a very minimum, healthcare providers need an in-depth orientation in the values and belief systems of minority patients, particularly as it relates to palliative care. It is important that this orientation be conducted by persons who are representative of the minority culture who can translate the unspoken values and perceptions that come into play.

Secondly, we should develop an extensive physician education program that allows physicians to explore the role of religion/spirituality and how those values can often conflict with the values of medicine and psychology can play an important part in that process. I also believe that there is a clear need for research that compares and contrasts the values of medicine with the values of religion, particularly as it relates to the meaning of life, and then additional research to explore how addressing the difference in values can lead to greater understanding.

Third, because African-American patients often seek out African-American physicians who agree with their mistrust and suspicion of palliative care, there is a need to develop more palliative care training programs geared toward African-Americans and other minority physicians so that these physicians will begin to understand and appreciate the true value of care that does not see curative treatment as the ultimate goal. . . .

Fourth, we need to work to revamp the Medicare system to allow reimbursement for palliative care in order to remove the stigma attached to the more traditional hospice benefit provision, specifically the 6-month prognosis provision.[1]

Fifth, we need to initiate a broad-based public education program to inform persons about the real limitations of aggressive medical treatment and how palliative/hospice care is often the most humane approach to care at the end of life. This effort needs to be culturally sensitive and include materials that are specifically designed to reach members of the minority communities.

Finally, let me say that from all of my years of experience with hospice, what I have learned is that patients and families are generally very grateful for the care that they receive be-

---

1. Hospice benefits are available to patients with a prognosis that they have six months or less to live.

cause of the incredible level of support that it provides. Most families that have experienced this care are amazed at how peaceful a Hospice death can be and express their desire to have a similarly peaceful death surrounded by their loved ones. They especially appreciate the wide variety of support that they receive from the many professional disciplines that are there to assist them, not only the medical professionals like the doctor, the nurse and the home health aide, but especially those disciplines that address the psychosocial concerns, the social wonder, the chaplain and the volunteer. Patients and families recognize that this is a wonderful model designed to speak to the body, mind and spirit. I have also been told by patients that they especially appreciate what they describe as an unconditional love and that they were amazed to experience the trust, respect and appreciation that many have never received from the healthcare system before. This is the kind of experience that can go a long way to overcoming the mistrust and suspicion that often characterizes the experience of the minority at the end of life.

*"We are somehow not paying attention to the whole person in the care of dying patients and bereaved people, because of our strong Western medical model."*

# Care for the Dying Is Inadequate in Western Society

Julia Neuberger

There need to be changes in the way Western society treats the dying, argues Rabbi Julia Neuberger in the following viewpoint. In Neuberger's opinion, Western medicine provides insufficient care for the terminally ill because it fails to consider the whole person. In addition to attending to the physical needs of the dying, asserts Neuberger, medical personnel should also consider patients' spiritual and emotional needs. Neuberger is author of *Caring for Dying People of Different Faiths* and chief executive of the King's Fund, an independent charitable organization that works to improve health care.

As you read, consider the following questions:

1. According to Neuberger, what has been revealed about end-of-life care from applications for grants from a variety of organizations?
2. How do Jews and Muslims differ from Christians in their views about end-of-life care, according to the author?
3. In the opinion of Richard Chartres, what is an important reason why people in Western societies find it so difficult to help the dying and the bereaved?

Julia Neuberger, "A Healthy View of Dying," *British Medical Journal*, vol. 327, July 26, 2003, p. 207. Copyright © 2003 by the British Medical Association. Reproduced by permission.

In his president's lecture for the King's Fund in June this year [2003] Richard Chartres, the bishop of London drew attention to our society's inability to see life and health holistically (lecture available on the King's Fund website, www.kingsfund.org). He took us back to ancient Pergamon [a Greek city] and its Temple of the Divine Healer, Aesculapius,[1] and gave us an insight into that hospital: "In the Greek medical tradition, the fundamental recipe for healthy living was 'know thyself and be moderate in all things,' and this outlook was expressed in the regime followed in the hospital . . . the temple must have been a tranquil and beautiful environment in which to recover, in an atmosphere that was a cross between Champneys and an Oxbridge college.[2]. . . It was in the ruins of this place that I can remember contemplating the theme of healthy living and healthy dying."

## Failure to Consider the Whole Person

The whole person was considered: mind, body, and spirit were as one. In the discussion that followed his lecture, a groundswell of feeling grew that, as a society, we are somehow not paying attention to the whole person in the care of dying patients and bereaved people, because of our strong Western medical model. Part by part, specialty by specialty, no integrated view can develop of the person and the culture from which he or she comes.

At the King's Fund, we had already been aware of a growing concern about this, from application for grants from a variety of organisations. Some wanted to do work on "natural burials" and different kinds of funerals. Others wanted specialist palliative care services for people from various ethnic and religious minorities. Some wanted a well trained group of "sitters" for dying people, so that relatives could have some respite. Others wanted to explore palliative care for conditions other than cancer, motor neurone disease, and AIDS. Time and again, we were being asked for help. As part of our response, we published a short paper on psycho-

1. the god of medicine and healing in ancient Greek mythology 2. Champneys College is an English college of health and beauty. "Oxbridge" refers to Oxford and Cambridge universities in England, two of the most famous and prestigious in the world.

logical support for dying people last year [2002], which received an enormous amount of attention.

## Shortcomings in Palliative Care Services

The degree of concern we have noted and the large number of grant applications we have received, plus the start of a campaign after Richard Chartres' lecture, suggest there is widespread unease with the Western medical approach to dying. Despite the huge advances made by the hospice movement and general advances in palliative care, in which Britain has undoubtedly taken a lead, the care available for terminally ill people is far from adequate, and far from satisfactory for a range of groups in our society—elderly people who do not have cancer, people with end stage renal failure, those with heart disease, those with Alzheimer's disease, black people, Muslims, Jews, Buddhists, Chinese, and so on. Meanwhile hospices worry increasingly about funding for the excellent work that they already do. Despite several national [British] attempts to encourage primary care and hospital services to provide better care at the end of life, services are patchy, depending too much on individual enthusiasts. There is no deeply rooted ethical base in medical practice about giving care when cure is no longer possible.

Many conditions once thought terminal are now chronic—people live for decades with cancer, heart disease, and AIDS—and their treatment raises no questions because they are seen as fitting into a curative model rather than a care model. Once they are seen as terminal cases, however, things change. Services can be quite brilliant, and totally culturally appropriate—as I found with both my parents, when they were dying. Equally, and particularly for people with Alzheimer's disease living in nursing homes, palliative care can be virtually non-existent, and spiritual pain goes completely unrecognised.

Exacerbating this inequality in service are the different views of different faiths and cultures on how hard one should strive to keep alive. Jews and Muslims, for instance, tend to argue for doing everything to keep people alive, life itself being seen as the most precious divine gift. Many Christian groups are less concerned with length of life than with last rites and final absolution. Chinese customs vary, and different minorities, apparently of the same group religion as the majority population, nevertheless have different views and customs that need to be respected. The experience is patchy, to say the least.

## Barriers to Good End-of-Life Care

Although there are few human experiences as profound and universal as the end of life, we are only beginning to create a health care system that will allow people to die as they wish, with dignity and with as little pain as possible. The challenges to creating that system are attitudinal, financial, clinical, and emotional. Despite increasing public discussion about end-of-life care, many people are uncomfortable thinking about their own deaths or the deaths of those they love. Talking openly about this is even harder. Beyond emotional barriers lie practical ones. Doctors, nurses, and social workers are not trained well in managing pain and addressing the patient's and family's emotional and spiritual needs. Long-time habits of thoughts and action are difficult to change—doctors are focused on curing rather than caring. Hospitals and nursing homes need additional staff and frequently face cutbacks and staff turnover.

Gary L. Stein, *Health and Social Work*, February 2004.

This raises huge questions about our healthcare system. Do the views of the people who are dying take precedence over the views of the service providers? An autonomy model would suggest that they do, but, if there is no advance directive, can one be sure? And, if the study of different attitudes to death is not mandatory for all healthcare professionals, how can we be sure that some attitudes will be recognised, let alone respected? Add to that a potent fear of death among young healthcare providers, many of whom will not have seen someone die before they became a doctor or nurse and for whom death is not the norm, and we have a recipe for problems.

## Time for a Change in Attitude

To quote Richard Chartres again: "Our failure to face our own fear of death is an important reason why we find it so difficult to help the dying and the bereaved . . . We try to gloss over the fact of death by using euphemisms and are protecting ourselves very often when we exclude children from funeral services or even the sight of dead bodies. Our hectic style of life owes much to the suppressed fear of death and the unexamined notion that the faster we live, the more we shall get out of this short life . . .

Hospices are places where we can experience and experiment with a different way of healthy living and healthy dying . . . medical intervention is subservient to exploring the potential in dying for health—health defined as the sustaining and development of a personal identity nourished by the resources and challenges of the environment and, most importantly, our multidimensional relationships."

## Establishing Principles

Yet we do not, and cannot, all die in hospices. Nor do all hospices succeed in providing this kind of healthy death. So some principles need to be established, as part of the value system of healthcare institutions. Among them needs to be a respect for varying cultural and religious attitudes, including a respect for secularism, which may require a different approach again. The desire of staff in hospices and palliative care teams to learn more about other faiths, and the need for textbooks about caring for dying people of many religions and ethnic groups, suggests a concern bubbling up from local communities and faith groups that is relatively new. Spirituality, most associated with death and dying, though often wrongly, has come back into fashion (some would say it never left).

[Baroness] Ilora Finlay argues that "just as perinatal mortality is a marker of nutrition and public health as well as of perinatal services, the care of our dying is an indicator that reflects the overall quality of our care and compassion." She is right. But that care needs to be multidimensional and generous, recognising the health that lies in dying well, and understanding that people differ in how they think about death and dying and that respect for those differences goes a long way to making people feel whole.

*"Of the thousands of papers published on end-of-life care in the last decade, only a few have addressed end-of-life care in developing countries."*

# End-of-Life Care in Developing Nations Has Not Been Adequately Addressed

Peter A. Singer and Kerry W. Bowman

In the following viewpoint Peter A. Singer and Kerry W. Bowman argue that while the majority of the world's deaths occur in developing nations, end-of-life care in these countries has not been adequately addressed. According to Singer and Bowman, Western approaches to end-of-life care often do not benefit the terminally ill in developing nations because of differences in culture and in causes of death. For example, while people in the West are relatively comfortable talking about death as as a failure of the body's organs to function, such a discussion would distress the terminally ill in many developing nations, who view death as ordained by God. Singer and Bowman are bioethicists at the University of Toronto Joint Centre of Bioethics in Ontario, Canada.

As you read, consider the following questions:

1. What percentage of yearly worldwide deaths occurs in developing countries, according to the authors?
2. How does the perception of illness differ in Western and non-Western cultures, as explained by the authors?

Peter A. Singer and Kerry W. Bowman, "Quality End-of-Life Care: A Global Perspective," *BMC Palliative Care*, vol. 1, July 25, 2002. www.biomedcentral. com/1472-684x/1/4. Copyright © 2002 by Singer and Bowman; licensee BioMed Central Ltd. Reproduced by permission.

There are 56 million deaths per year in the world, 85% of which are in developing countries. . . .

It is ironic therefore that of the thousands of papers published on end-of-life care in the last decade, only a few have addressed end-of-life care in developing countries. This is perhaps nothing more than another manifestation of the 90/10 gap—that 90% of medical research is undertaken on those diseases that cause 10% of the global burden of disease. . . .

This gap is important to note since applying strategies and concepts from developed onto developing countries may be inappropriate simply because of the epidemiological context of death, let alone the cultural differences which we address in the next section. The context of deaths in developed and developing countries are different, and context matters in end-of-life care. . . .

## Different Causes of Death

Causes of death differ between developed and developing countries. According to estimates in WHO's [World Health Organization's] World Health Report 2000, the five leading causes of death in sub-Saharan Africa are HIV/AIDS (2,154,000), acute lower respiratory infections (1,073,000), malaria (953,000), diarrhoeal diseases (765,000), and measles (514,000). Over half the deaths in these countries are attributable to infectious and parasitic diseases. In fact, infectious diseases are responsible for almost half of mortality in developing countries throughout the world. And, approximately half of infectious disease mortality can be attributed to just three diseases—HIV/AIDS, TB [tuberculosis], and malaria. These three diseases cause over 300 million illnesses and more than 5 million deaths each year. . . .

In the countries which make up the lowest mortality stratum in North America (Canada, Cuba and U.S.). . . . More than 65% of deaths are attributable to some form of cancer or cardiovascular disease. Whereas a mere 2% of deaths are attributable to infectious diseases.

In the last hundred years and with particular concentration in recent decades, the West has seen a significant shift from death occurring from infectious diseases to death occurring from degenerative conditions occurring late in life. These changes have lengthened both life and the dying trajectory. In the developing world death is often a faster process and occurs earlier in life. For example, in Africa, infant mortality is close to 10%, and an average of 151 of every 1,000 children die before age five, according to World Bank statistics. Although AIDS is an affliction well known in Western health care, it is a more brisk, debilitating illness in developing countries. The lived experience of people in the developed world is that of death occurring largely in old age as opposed to the developing world in which a high proportion of preventable deaths occur in childhood and early adult life.

## Life Expectancy Is Decreasing in Some Developing Nations

Examining recent data one may assume that the global picture for health—and by implication for end-of-life care—is encouraging. In 1955, the world average of life expectancy was 48 years; by 1995 it had risen to 65 years. However, this positive trend masks the fact that improvements are not universal. In 16 countries, life expectancy declined between 1975–1995. In much of sub-Saharan Africa, AIDS, in combination with declining economies and health care delivery systems, is having a powerful effect on health, the nature and experience of dying, and life expectancy. In Uganda, for example, AIDS is the leading cause of death in young adults, and life expectancy between 1995–2000 was 32.7 years. Seven countries in sub-Saharan Africa now have life expectancies below 40 years by 2010, 11 countries are expected to have life expectancies near 30 years.

It is easy to make too much of the differences in causes of death in developed and developing countries. We do not want to enter into those debates here. Rather, we simply want to sound a cautionary note. Strategies to improve end-of-life care depend on context including the patterns of death, this context varies around the world, and these contextual features must be taken into account to enhance the opportunities for success of any concepts and strategies to improve end-of-life care.

Because culture significantly influences how we see the world, any effort to understand or improve quality end-of-life care in the world must be sensitive to cultural consider-ations. Cultures are much deeper than their traditions, ex-tending to fundamental differences in modes of reasoning grounded in the way the world is perceived. Furthermore, it is known that attitudes toward end-of-life care is relative to particular cultures, societies, and times. Often, when people planning or providing health care and recipients of health care come from different cultural backgrounds, they interact under the influence of unspoken assumptions that are so dif-ferent that they prevent effective communication and initia-tives may break down all together. Simply applying Western perspective on end-of-life care to developing nations is un-realistic, and apt to fail.

## The Impact of AIDS

Seven countries in sub-Saharan Africa have life expectancies of less than 40 years of age. In Botswana, for example, life ex-pectancy is only 39 years, while it would have been 72, if it were not for AIDS. This means that the majority of Botswanans on average will live 30 years less than they would have if not for the AIDS pandemic.

This trend is also seen in Asia and Latin America and the Caribbean although due to lower HIV prevalence levels, the impact is not as great. In Haiti, life expectancy is now 51, while it would have been 59, if it were not for AIDS. In Asia, Thailand, Cambodia and Burma have lost between two and five years of life expectancy.

U.S. Agency for International Development, 2002.

Although Western culture is diverse . . . and increasingly views health and illness in a broader context, Western medicine remains largely based on scientific, rational and objective principles. Ultimately this is as much a cultural construction as any non-Western philosophic or health-re-lated belief system. Disease is perceived as being largely un-der the control of science. Because of the institutionalization of death, many people may expect medical solutions at the end-of-life. Death is often perceived as a failure of medical care. Demand for aggressive treatment at the end-of-life can become extreme and unrealistic. Research in North America shows that 18 per cent of lifetime costs for medical care are apt to be incurred in the last year of life. . . .

## Different Views of Death in Developing Nations

Many people in developing countries hold profoundly different views of the nature, cause and meaning of health, illness, death and dying than those in the developed world. . . . In Western medicine, the primary explanatory model of illness focuses on abnormalities in the structure and function of body organs and systems. Most non-Western cultures tend to perceive illness in a much broader and far less tangible manner—for example, some Africans may perceive health and disease as separate entities, influenced by external forces such as witchcraft, revenge or other social causes. These belief systems are often referred to as traditional belief systems. . . .

For many people in developing countries stronger religious and cultural observances and community support may ameliorate much of the need or expectation for "specialized" approaches to end-of-life care. In many societies in the developing world many people are barely exposed to other views—traditional beliefs of death being the will of God or a natural consequence of the cycle of life may be profoundly comforting and nurture a fatalistic acceptance and stoicism toward death. Introducing death as a "specialized" service— by viewing suffering as a treatable, medical phenomenon— raises a profound ethical question as to whether it . . . would be at odds with existing cultural and religious perspectives on suffering, death and their meaning.

The health care infrastructure of some developing countries may be minimal, and focused on disease prevention. Discussions of death, in this context, may be shunned as they are a reminder of the gross inadequacies of the health care system. As with Western nations effective pain control is problematic, although the roots of the problem are different. In developing nations pain control is impeded by a lack of opioids and a fear of Western style drug problems, which may greatly limit the use of analgesics.

These cultural considerations lead to the conclusion that any effort to improve quality of end-of-life care in developing countries must be carefully tailored, and include people from developing countries, who will be sensitive to the cultural context. . . .

## Western Approaches to End-of-Life Care Are Inappropriate

Health care initiatives in the developing world must deal with inadequate infrastructures, poor administrative systems, the extreme poverty of many patients, restricted opioid prescribing and minimal educational opportunities for health care staff. Clearly, these are not the conditions for building specialized programs. Aggressive high-tech approaches at the end-of-life are not feasible. A further impediment to improving end-of-life care in the developing world is that a majority of health care spending, both public and private, goes to curative efforts—hospitals in urban areas often account for more than 80% of total health care costs. Although changing quickly, the majority of the population in the developing world continues to live in rural areas. . . .

Death in the developing world is most often seen as integral part of life. Consequently, the Western "specialization" of death may already be a contributing factor to why traditional Western approaches to end-of-life care have had so little effect in the developing world. Integrating local, culturally based perspectives of health, illness and dying in combination with building national consensus to changes in policies, and procedures, are apt to have a greater effect on improving end-of-life care in the developing world than implementing contemporary Western medical advances.

# Periodical Bibliography

The following articles have been selected to supplement the diverse views presented in this chapter.

| | |
|---|---|
| *Business Week* | "Giving More Patients 'A Good Death,'" November 20, 2000. |
| *Cancer Weekly* | "Hospice May Not Be Right for All Patients," December 3, 2002. |
| Jean Chatzky | "A Will for the Living: How to Make Your Wishes Known, in Case You Can't Speak for Yourself," *Time*, November 3, 2003. |
| Carrie Click | "Hospice: For One Family Dealing with Dying, the Natural Choice," *Glenwood Springs Post Independent*, April 26, 2004. |
| Angela Fagerlin and Carl E. Schneider | "Living Wills: Not a Be-All and End-All," *Los Angeles Times*, November 12, 2003. |
| Vida Foubister | "Palliative Care: Mainstream Model," *American Medical News*, February 26, 2001. |
| August Gribbin | "We Shall Not Fear . . ." *Insight on the News*, February 26, 2001. |
| Bruce Jennings et al. | "Access to Hospice Care: Expanding Boundaries, Overcoming Barriers," *Hastings Center Report*, March/April 2003. |
| Barron H. Lerner | "Planning for the Long Goodbye," *New York Times*, June 18, 2004. |
| Michael Rybarski | "Boomers After All Is Said and Done," *American Demographics*, June 1, 2004. |
| Gary L. Stein | "Improving Our Care at Life's End: Making a Difference," *Health and Social Work*, February 2004. |
| James M. Thunder | "Quiet Killings in Medical Facilities: Detection & Prevention," *Issues in Law & Medicine*, Spring 2003. |
| Elizabeth Tong et al. | "What Is a Good Death?: Minority and Non-Minority Perpectives," *Journal of Palliative Care*, Autumn 2003. |

# CHAPTER 2

# How Should the Physical Pain of Terminal Illness Be Relieved?

# Chapter Preface

Abigail Burroughs was diagnosed with cancer at age nineteen. By 2001, at just twenty-one years old, she was dying as the disease spread through her head and neck. Conventional treatments had failed to halt the cancer, but her doctor felt that two experimental drugs—not yet approved by the U.S. Food and Drug Administration (FDA) and thus not available to the public—had a very significant chance of helping her. Abigail's parents begged the manufacturers to give Abigail the drugs, but without success. On June 9, 2001, Abigail passed away. Her father, Frank Burroughs, believes these drugs might have saved her life. "We tried to get Abigail into narrowly defined clinical trials," he explains, "but she did not qualify for them. We worked very hard to acquire the drugs on a compassionate basis and got nowhere. . . . We did not get a chance to try to save dear, sweet, talented, compassionate Abigail."

The Burroughs are not alone in their experience. Many people in the United States believe that the terminally ill should have access to experimental drugs if there is a chance that these drugs might improve, or even save, their lives. They argue that since these people are dying anyway, the use of experimental drugs is essentially without risk. Attorney Jonathan W. Emord argues that someone who is dying has the right to try anything that might save his or her life. He argues,

> Imagine for a moment a horrible circumstance. Imagine that you . . . are stricken with an incurable brain tumor. Imagine that you have undergone surgery and several rounds of chemo and radiation therapy to no avail. Your doctors have told you they can do nothing more. They predict you will not live past six months to a year. . . . What on earth can you do? You are left with two very basic choices. You can accept the conventional wisdom and prepare to die, or you can fight for life against all odds and on your own terms. If you are like my clients, you will fight with every ounce of strength you can muster. You will race against time and the ravages of disease to find and try every promising experimental drug available for your condition.

Drug companies, however, argue that giving unapproved drugs to terminally ill patients is costly and can actually slow down the approval process. According to Dr. Sue Hellman, the chief medical officer and senior vice president of the pharmaceutical company Genentech, the company only produces enough of an experimental drug for the patients in the clinical trials. Supplying the drug outside controlled trials is very costly, she argues. Drug companies are often reluctant to admit terminally ill patients to their trials because FDA rules require them to include all patients' results in statistics of a drug's performance. Including terminally ill patients who die during the trial would make the drug appear to be ineffective, even dangerous, the drug makers say, delaying FDA approval.

As the debate over experimental drugs illustrates, treating pain in terminally ill patients often results in heated debate. The authors in the following chapter debate several contentious pain management approaches.

*"At present most patients have a pain free death. A significant minority, however, do not."*

# Effective Pain Relief Is Hampered by Inadequate Knowledge

Julia Riley

All terminally ill patients have different responses to pain medication, asserts Julia Riley in the following viewpoint, and doctors do not currently have the knowledge to effectively treat every different case. As a result, she claims, a significant number of terminally ill patients do not receive adequate pain medication. These patients, says Riley, frequently spend the end of their lives in a great deal of pain, causing extreme distress to themselves and their friends and families. She advocates increased research on ways to more effectively relieve pain in the terminally ill. Riley is a consultant in palliative medicine at the Royal Marsden Hospital in London.

As you read, consider the following questions:
1. What memories did the author's nephews have of their mother's death?
2. Why is it often difficult to adequately assess pain, in Riley's opinion?
3. According to the author, in what percentage of patients does morphine cause either intolerable or adverse effects?

My sister in law died of metastatic malignant melanoma five years ago [in 1998], leaving behind a six year old boy, a four year old boy, and a pair of 10 month old twins. My recollection of her last weeks is pain, pain, and more pain.

## Memories of Pain

A year after her death the family attended a bereavement weekend at Winston's Wish—a charity that supports bereaved children and young adults—in Gloucestershire [in Great Britain]. Winston's Wish offers young people support and information to help them understand what has happened, slowly allowing them to learn to live with their loss. The charity has worked with over 2000 young people [between 1992 and 2003].

The charity workers' greatest skill is in encouraging children to communicate non-verbally. On their weekend the children were asked to colour sand and pour it into a test tube. Each colour had a particular meaning. The children were asked to write on a piece of paper what the colour meant to them, with reference to the person who had died. They were also asked to write on a porcelain plate anything that had made them angry about their loss. They then threw the plate in the bin, listening to it as it shattered. My four year old nephew coloured his sand red. He explained that the red was the "PAIN." My eldest nephew wrote PAIN on his plate and shattered it. In the discussions that followed both boys were able to articulate their memories of the screaming that came out of their mother's room as she was dying. My brother corroborated their memories: he recalled that every time she screamed she was given more diamorphine. After each dose of diamorphine she either slept or became paranoid.

There was no real analgesia, only sedation and side effects. Why? It is a question that has plagued me ever since. Here she was being cared for by a good palliative care service in London, experts in WHO's [World Health Organization's] "analgesic ladder."[1] Yet, if you now ask any member

---

1. This ladder helps doctors select the most appropriate drug for the intensity of the pain.

of the family whether she had a good, pain free death, the answer will be a categorical "no." Pain is multifactorial. It is impossible for relatives of patients—even when doctors—to objectively assess their pain. I was a newly qualified consultant in palliative care at the time, and my memory of complete impotence remains. Over the years since my sister in law's death I have come to realise that her experience is not the norm. I have, however, seen other people whose pain has been equally difficult to control.

---

## Common Misconceptions About Pain

• Physical or behavioral signs of pain (e.g., abnormal vital signs, grimacing, limping) are more reliable indicators of pain than patient self-report.
• Elderly or cognitively impaired patients cannot use pain intensity rating scales.
• Pain does not exist in the absence of physical or behavioral signs or detectable tissue damage.
• Pain without an obvious physical cause, or that is more severe than expected based on findings, is usually psychogenic.
• Comparable stimuli produce the same level of pain in all individuals (i.e., a uniform pain threshold exists).
• Prior experience with pain teaches a person to be more tolerant of pain.
• Analgesics should be withheld until the cause of the pain is established.
• Noncancer pain is not as severe as cancer pain.
• Patients who are knowledgeable about pain medications, are frequent emergency department patrons, or have been taking opioids for a long time are necessarily addicts or "drug seekers."
• Use of opioids in patients with pain will cause them to become addicted.
• Patients who respond to a placebo drug are malingering.
• Neonates, infants, and young children have decreased pain sensation.

American Pain Society, 2004.

---

Looking back, I wonder whether some patients just did not respond to morphine. This has been shown to be the case for codeine: 6–7% of white people do not respond to this drug. Genetic variation can be a powerful factor in pain relief. It is reported that between 10% and 30% of patients treated with oral morphine have either intolerable adverse effects or are inadequately treated, or both. The reason for this variability has not yet been shown.

Today, many more analgesic drugs are available. Opioid switching—changing from morphine to an alternative opioid—is gaining popularity in pain management. Its aim is to improve a patient's response to analgesics and to reduce adverse side effects.

## The Right to a Pain Free Death

At present most patients have a pain free death. A significant minority, however, do not. It is for such patients that research is needed. The goal would be to identify patients who do not respond to morphine, before analgesia is given, and then to find an effective alternative analgesic.

Research has begun. My hope is that in the future a good, pain free death can be the right of everyone, so that other people do not have to go through the extreme distress suffered by my late sister in law, my brother, and their boys.

> *"Complex and rigid regulations coupled with tough sanctions can effectively deter physicians from treating pain adequately."*

# Effective Pain Relief Is Hampered by Drug Control Laws

Carol Sieger

While physicians have the knowledge to adequately relieve pain in terminally ill patients, the law often prevents them from doing so, argues Carol Sieger in the following viewpoint. In some states, doctors who administer high doses of pain medication that contribute to respiratory failure can be criminally prosecuted. Sieger believes that legal and regulatory barriers need to be reduced so that doctors are not afraid to provide their patients with effective doses of analgesics. Sieger is deputy director of the Center to Advance Palliative Care, an organization that works to develop and improve palliative care programs.

As you read, consider the following questions:

1. In Sieger's opinion, how does the possibility of an investigation affect the willingness of a physician to prescribe strong narcotics?
2. Why must changes in the law address pharmacists in addition to doctors, according to the author?
3. On what health care provider responsibility did *Estate of Henry James v. Hillhaven Corp.* focus, according to Sieger?

Carol Sieger, "Pain Management: The Role of the Law," www.partnershipfor caring.org, September 2000. Originally appeared in *Choice in Dying News*, vol. 6, no. 4, Winter 1997. This version updated in 2000 by Partnership for Caring. Reproduced by permission of the author.

Although today's technology can alleviate most severe pain, studies show that many terminally ill people still die in pain. Pain management would seem to be a medical issue, not a legal one. However, the law plays a significant role in how well a patient's pain is managed, not only because of what the law actually says, but also because of what providers believe it says, even though their understanding may be incorrect. Providers' understanding of the law, combined with other obstacles to good pain management, results in large numbers of patients whose pain is inadequately treated.

## Legal Barriers

Federal and state drug control laws intensely regulate the prescribing of controlled substances (such as morphine or other opioids) that are used to manage pain. All practice-oriented drug law and regulation is based on the federal Controlled Substances Act of 1970. The Act regulates drugs or substances that are subject to, or have the potential for, abuse or physical or psychological dependence. All healthcare providers who deal with controlled substances are subject to the Controlled Substances Act and the drug control laws and regulations of the state in which they are licensed and practicing. A physician who violates these laws or regulations can be vulnerable to investigation and criminal prosecution. Although it is rare that a physician is ever prosecuted, even the possibility of an investigation can significantly inhibit a physician's willingness to provide the quantities of strong narcotics necessary to relieve some severe pain.

One goal of regulatory and law enforcement agencies is to prevent the fraudulent prescribing and dispensing of controlled substances. Agencies use many measures to pursue this goal including strict reporting requirements and restrictions on the quantity of drugs that can be dispensed at one time. For example, regulations in some states limit the number of tablets to be prescribed at one time, hampering a physician's ability to prescribe a sufficient level of pain medications and requiring the patient to obtain multiple prescriptions each week.

Some states require that multiple copies of a prescription be submitted to the appropriate agencies as a way of monitoring physicians' prescribing practices. A 1987 U.S. Department of Justice study of states with multiple-copy prescription requirements showed a greater than 50 percent reduction in prescriptions for regulated drugs, such as morphine, which are necessary to control moderate to severe pain. Surveys in Texas and New York suggest that this increased regulatory oversight reduced the number of legitimate prescriptions for controlled drugs. The requirements resulted in an increased use of drugs less suitable for the conditions under treatment, but they did not decrease fraudulently-written prescriptions. Complex and rigid regulations coupled with tough sanctions can effectively deter physicians from treating pain adequately.

## Professional Sanctions

Professional organizations such as state medical boards can also impede effective pain management. These boards monitor physician practice, and they have the authority to investigate and bring a disciplinary action against a physician who fails to meet an acceptable level of conduct. If a state board believes, even erroneously, that the physician is violating appropriate prescribing practices, it can bring disciplinary action against that physician. Although the number of actual investigations and disciplinary actions is low, the threat alone can be sufficient to discourage physicians from effectively treating patients' pain. This dampening effect on pain management is especially troubling because many of the physicians who are members of state boards improperly interpret existing laws and are themselves ignorant about pain management techniques and the large dosages that can be required to effectively manage some types of pain effectively. For example, some boards continue to evaluate physicians' prescribing practices in terms of dosage and length of treatment. However, such indicators are not useful for separating inappropriate or fraudulent prescription practices from good pain management.

## Removing Legal and Regulatory Barriers to Pain Management

To respond to the need to improve pain management, states must evaluate their laws and regulations on physicians' abil-

Laws and regulations must provide protection for health professionals to aggressively treat pain with analgesic drugs, and when needed, with terminal sedation, even if these treatments hasten death. At present, physicians and nurses are often reluctant to give large doses of analgesics to dying patients, fearing that they will be subject to prosecution if the drugs contribute to a respiratory arrest. Regulations must specify that an intent to relieve pain, supported by documentation of the patient's report of pain or behaviors that suggest pain (e.g., grimacing or moaning), can justify the use of high doses of analgesics or sedatives, even if these treatments also depress respiration or hasten death in some other way. Such treatment is based on ethical principles that are widely accepted by health professionals and ethicists and should not be considered an act of assisted suicide or euthanasia.

American Pain Society, 2004.

ity and willingness to prescribe effective pain medications. As of September 1997, 16 states have passed what are called intractable pain statutes. (Intractable pain is defined as severe pain that has not been alleviated by reasonable efforts.)[1] These acts recognize that in some cases controlled substances are indispensable for the treatment of pain and that the appropriate drug dosage will vary from individual to individual. States such as California, Minnesota, Missouri, Nevada, North Dakota, Oregon and Texas have passed statutes which specifically state that a physician shall not be subject to disciplinary action for prescribing or administering controlled substances in the course of treatment for intractable pain. Statutes and the issuance of rules that have the force of law can give physicians some reassurance that their justifiable use of proper pain management techniques will not result in legal sanctions.

## Model Pain Relief Act

Model legislation has been developed to aid legislators designing or amending state laws dealing with intractable pain. The Project on Legal Constraints on Access to Effective Pain

1. In 2004, 21 states had passed these statutes.

Relief conducted a major research effort to provide guidance to the various states considering the matter. Funded by the Mayday Fund and the Emily Davie and Joseph S. Kornfeld Foundation, the project analyzed the legal issues, regulatory mechanisms, and education and training of physicians that seemed to impede effective pain management. One of the results of this research effort was the development of a model state statute called the Pain Relief Act. The objective of this model act is to prevent unnecessary investigation, protracted proceedings, and inappropriate legal sanctions against healthcare providers. The presumption is that physicians may be less likely to undertreat pain when their fears of protracted proceedings or litigation are alleviated.

Changes in the law must address the concerns of other healthcare providers, such as nurses and pharmacists, who also handle controlled substances. For example, pharmacists have a corresponding responsibility with physicians and are co-liable for prescriptions written for patients. Regulatory measures are complex and cumbersome because of the volume of recordkeeping provisions that state and federal agencies require. Failure by pharmacists and other healthcare providers to keep accurate records can result in a $25,000 fine. The model Pain Relief Act addresses issues faced by all healthcare providers who deal with controlled substances, *not* just physicians.

## Case Law Developments

Decisions in two cases may represent the beginning of a trend in affirming a patient's right to proper pain control and in assigning liability for failure to provide adequate pain relief. In one [1989] case, *State v. McAfee*, the Georgia Supreme Court found not only that Mr. McAfee, a quadriplegic, had the right to have his ventilator disconnected, but that his right to be free from pain at the time of the ventilator's disconnection was inseparable from his right to refuse medical treatment. In *Estate of Henry James v. Hillhaven Corp.* [1990] a nurse and the nurse's employer, a nursing home, decided to substitute pain medication for a resident with metastatic prostate cancer against his doctor's orders, leaving the patient in agony. This lawsuit focused on the healthcare provider's responsibility to ensure the proper administration of pain medications, and a North Carolina jury awarded $15 million in damages. The $15 million jury verdict was resolved by settlement among the parties for an undisclosed amount.

## Other Important Changes

Although improving laws and regulations can remove some of the barriers to good pain management, these changes alone will not result in improved pain management. We need to address many other obstacles as well, most importantly the lack of knowledge among healthcare providers. They need to know more about how to assess patient's pain effectively and about the specific strategies and techniques required to treat pain. They also need accurate information and education about the laws and regulations that affect prescribing; otherwise improving the quality of laws and regulations will be of no benefit. In addition, we need to address the widespread myths about psychological addiction to narcotics in relation to pain management.

The U.S. Department of Health and Human Services Agency for Healthcare Policy and Research has stated that "[t]he ethical obligation to manage pain and relieve the patient's suffering is at the core of a healthcare professional's commitment." Yet to date [2000] it does not appear that medical schools have subscribed to that view. Many medical schools offer insufficient education about effective pain management. In one survey of 81 resident physicians, the majority were unable to answer survey questions that were considered to demonstrate reasonable knowledge in the area of pain control. In the same survey, a review of the curriculum at 55 medical schools showed that only eight offered a course in cancer pain management. If we are to fully address the issue of unrelieved pain, it is crucial that physicians receive education in current pain management techniques, not only in medical school but through continuing education. Without this knowledge, physicians will be unable to judge the safety and effectiveness of certain pain medications, and the likely outcome is that they will undertreat pain in many of their patients.

Pain is a complex phenomenon that involves a physical response to injury or disease, which can be affected by emotional, social, spiritual, and economic forces. Proper control of pain for all patients will require changes in the law, education and disciplinary proceedings, and in how the medical community views its role in the proper treatment of pain. The increased national focus on the care of people who are dying has brought the issue of proper pain management into bold relief. But to ensure that increased attention to the issue results in real change, the public must continue to demand that its policymakers, educators and medical providers address the many obstacles to effective pain management. Patients and their loved ones are entitled to expect that healthcare providers will manage pain properly.

*"When unacceptable suffering persists
despite standard palliative measures,
terminal sedation . . . [is an] imperfect but
useful last-resort."*

# Patients Should Be Allowed to Choose Terminal Sedation

Timothy E. Quill and Ira R. Byock

In the following viewpoint Timothy E. Quill and Ira R. Byock contend that terminal sedation—the practice of discontinuing nutrition and life support for terminally ill patients
while using sedatives to make them unconscious—should be
available as a last resort for the dying. They describe the case
of "BG" to illustrate the way terminal sedation can allow patients to die peacefully and painlessly. Quill is a doctor at the
University of Rochester Medical Center in New York, and
Byock is director of palliative medicine at the Dartmouth-
Hitchcock Medical Center in New Hampshire.

As you read, consider the following questions:

1. What was BG's treatment goal, according to Quill and
   Byock?
2. According to the authors, what percentage of hospice
   patients describe their pain as "severe" in the last week
   of life?
3. What is the difference between terminal sedation for
   patients expected to recover and terminal sedation for
   the dying, as explained by Quill and Byock?

P alliative care, which addresses the multiple physical, psychosocial, and spiritual dimensions of suffering, should
be the standard of care for the dying. Such care is usually effective but some patients develop intolerable suffering despite excellent care. This paper discusses terminal sedation
and voluntary refusal of hydration and nutrition as potential
last-resort responses to severe, unrelievable end-of-life suffering. As part of their palliative care skills and services, clinicians must have strategies for responding to the troubling
problems of patients who experience such suffering. These
two options provide a means of response for patients, families, and clinicians who oppose physician-assisted suicide.

## Case Presentation

*BG was a 66-year-old retired radiologist who developed a large
glioblastoma [brain tumor] in the left parietal lobe. After extensive discussion, he elected to pursue a purely symptom-oriented approach. BG was married with two grown children. He was a
proud, independent person who valued his intellectual abilities and
physical integrity. He was a lifelong Unitarian. From his experience as a radiologist, he knew the natural history and potential
burdens of aggressive treatment of similar brain tumors. He did
not want to die but was fearful of becoming physically dependent
and intellectually impaired.*

*The treatment goal was to manage his symptoms so that he
could have quality time with his wife and children. . . . Initially,
his right-side weakness and headache improved for several weeks
as he and his family worked to achieve closure in their lives together.*

*Unfortunately, BG abruptly developed right-side weakness and
intermittent confusion . . ., and his symptoms steadily worsened despite treatment. Sensing his physical and intellectual deterioration,
BG wanted to "get on with it before I can't do anything for myself." Further mental and physical deterioration became more
frightening to him than death. He hoped he could die quickly by
stopping [his medications]. BG's physician urged him to continue
his medications for symptom relief, but BG did not want to take
anything that could in any way prolong his life. At his internist's
insistence, BG agreed to a single visit with a psychiatrist, who confirmed that BG understood his treatment options and was not clin-*

*ically depressed. After saying his goodbyes to friends and family, BG discontinued [his medications].*

*To BG's consternation, he did not become comatose or die. Instead, his right-side weakness worsened and his seizures became more frequent. BG found his situation intolerable. He did not explicitly request medication that could be taken in a lethal dose, but his desire for a hastened death was clear. "I just want to go to sleep and not wake up," he said.*

*All members of the team were committed to relieving his distress but had different views about explicitly assisting death. They searched for common ground while continuing to adjust his seizure management, support his family, and bring some quality to his days. None of their efforts changed BG's certainty that he did not want to continue living under his current circumstances. . . .*

## The Clinical Problem

Comprehensive palliative care is highly effective, but survey data show that 5% to 35% of patients in hospice programs describe their pain as "severe" in the last week of life and that 25% describe their shortness of breath as "unbearable." On occasion, such symptoms as delirium, bleeding, weakness, open wounds, profound weight loss, and seizures challenge the most experienced hospice teams. . . .

*BG feared becoming a burden to his family and developing progressive loss of mental capacity more than he feared uncontrolled pain. He had no moral reservations about hastening death under his current circumstances. For him, the humaneness and effectiveness of the intervention were more important than whether it required his physician's "active" or "passive" assistance. His physician had moral and legal reservations about hastening death but was deeply committed to BG's comfort and wanted to be responsive to the dilemma that he faced.*

## Definition of Terminal Sedation

*Terminal sedation* is the use of high doses of sedatives to relieve extremes of physical distress. It is not restricted to end-of-life care and is sometimes used as a temporizing measure in trauma, burn, postsurgical, and intensive care. Although rendering a patient unconscious to escape suffering is an extraordinary measure, withholding such treatment in certain circumstances would be inhumane. Because most of the patients who receive heavy sedation are expected to recover, careful attention is paid to maintaining adequate ventilation, hydration, and nutrition.

## The Right Thing to Do

Good and caring physicians where adequate palliation cannot otherwise be achieved in a manner acceptable to the patient . . . knowingly and intentionally kill their dying patients with terminal sedation and dehydration, which is properly characterized as "palliative care of last resort." Yes, physicians (very rarely, thank goodness) must cause homicides. But these are excusable homicides, just as are homicides effected in self defense, in battle during war or by granting a mortally wounded intractably suffering comrade the grace of a *"coup de grace."* . . . This is simply the right thing to do in a total situational ethics context: it most fully affirms the worth of the dying patient and respects that patient's autonomy.

End-of-Life Choices–USA, 2001.

When applied to patients who have no substantial prospect of recovery, terminal sedation refers to a similar last-resort clinical response to extreme, unrelieved physical suffering. The purpose of the medications is to render the patient unconscious to relieve suffering, not to intentionally end his or her life. However, in the context of far-advanced disease and expected death, artificial nutrition, hydration, antibiotics, mechanical ventilation, and other life-prolonging interventions are not instituted and are usually withdrawn if they are already in place. These measures are withheld during terminal sedation because they could prolong the dying process without contributing to the quality of the patient's remaining life. In the context of end-of-life care, the component practices of intensive symptom management and withholding life-sustaining treatment have widespread ethical and legal support. . . .

*BG stopped eating and drinking. The initial week was physically comfortable and personally meaningful. BG's family shared stories, played cards, and listened to music. BG took antiseizure medications with sips of water but absolutely nothing else orally. Morphine . . . controlled his headaches without causing sedation.*

*His mouth was kept moist with ice chips and swabs, but he was careful not to swallow any of the liquid. After 9 days, he could be roused but spent most of the day and night sleeping. . . .*

## A Peaceful Death

*On day 10, BG became confused and agitated and began having hallucinations. The peace and comfort that he and his family had achieved began to unravel. BG was now incapable of informed consent but had previously given permission for sedation if this problem arose. . . . After several [doses of sedative], BG seemed to be sleeping comfortably. No attempt was made to restore consciousness, and no further increases in medication were needed to maintain sedation. . . .*

*BG died quietly approximately 24 hours later in his home, surrounded by his family. BG's family had remained resolute in their support for his decision and firmly committed to keeping him at home. However, they also continued to have emotional family discussions and at times struggled with whether they had done too little or too much to help him die peacefully. They drew comfort from recognizing that they had kept BG's values in the forefront and made the best of a potentially devastating situation.*

Medicine cannot sanitize dying or provide perfect solutions for all clinical dilemmas. When unacceptable suffering persists despite standard palliative measures, terminal sedation and voluntary refusal of food and fluids are imperfect but useful last-resort options that can be openly pursued. Patients and their families who fear that physicians will not respond to extreme suffering will be reassured when such options are predictably made available. Relevant professional bodies can help by adopting policy statements that attest to the ethical and professional acceptability of these components of palliative care.

*"Terminal sedation does not offer patients more control at the end of life. It offers only death."*

# Terminal Sedation Should Not Be Used in Palliative Care

Mark B. Blocher

Terminal sedation is the practice of using sedatives to cause unconsciousness in a terminally ill person, then discontinuing nutrition and other life support. In the following viewpoint Mark B. Blocher argues that terminal sedation is a form of killing that is morally wrong and violates the principles of hospice care. In addition, he asserts, acceptance of terminal sedation is dangerous because it could lead to the use of the procedure as a convenience and not as a last resort. Blocher is the publisher of the *Biblical Bioethics Advisor*, a journal that contains articles about current issues in bioethics.

As you read, consider the following questions:
1. What is the principle of "double effect," as explained by Blocher?
2. According to the author, how does terminal sedation undermine the core values of hospice?
3. How might the use of terminal sedation alter deathbed scenes, in Blocher's opinion?

[G reek philosopher] Socrates, is credited with having said, "Young men fear death; old men fear dying." Young men fear the loss of all they might have accomplished and experienced over a normal life span, while old men, having experienced whatever life had to offer them, fear the process of dying itself. In the modern age, where control and efficiency are crowning virtues, people fear dying alone, in pain, and being a burden on others. They fear the kind of dying process that modern medicine is capable of inducing.

The debates over legalizing physician assisted suicide and euthanasia have grown more intense in recent years, fueled by the dwindling influence of Judeo-Christian ethics, an aging population, and rising health care costs. Oregon already permits physician assisted suicide and Hawaii's legislature narrowly defeated a similar law by only three votes [in 2002].

Terminal sedation is portrayed as one way to reconcile objections to physician assisted suicide/euthanasia with demands for the maximum in comfort care. Proponents argue that it is an ethical and humane means of addressing the needs of the dying. Despite improvements in pain and symptom management for terminal patients, a small number continue to experience severe pain and other distressing symptoms that many would consider intolerable. Some caregivers believe terminal sedation is the best response. Terminal sedation is a term describing a form of end-of-life treatment that is gaining acceptance among both ethicists and physicians, partly because they view it as a valid alternative to physician-assisted suicide for patients whose pain and suffering cannot be relieved by existing pain management techniques. In this article, I will explore the nature of this form of palliative (comfort) care and discuss the ethical issues that it presents for the Christian medical practitioner, patients and families.

## Terminal Sedation Defined

Terminal sedation generally refers to the deliberate termination of a person's awareness through the use of drugs that induce deep sleep, and the withholding or withdrawal of life support technologies such as food and fluids. Terminal sedation places a person in virtually the same state as one who is under anesthesia before and during surgery. However, with terminal sedation, all supportive care is stopped and drugs are administered in an amount sufficient to make the patient unconscious and unaware. When instituted in this manner, terminal sedation results in the patient's death within a short period of time. This is why the procedure is called terminal. It is intended to produce death.

## Ethical Issues

The justification for using terminal sedation is the difficulty of effectively managing end-of-life symptoms that become increasingly unresponsive to standard medical interventions. Proponents of terminal sedation argue that such a death is desired by the patient (and welcomed by the family) because it releases the patient from a conscious awareness of his or her deteriorating condition. Opponents argue that terminal sedation is simply physician-assisted suicide by another name.

Perhaps the most obvious ethical question is this: Does terminal sedation represent a more benign-appearing form of killing, what some call "slow euthanasia?" Is the administration of terminal sedation to an imminently dying patient an act that deserves to be called killing? Does terminal sedation undermine the long-held tradition of hospice—that death should neither be hastened nor prolonged? May a Christian practitioner morally provide terminal sedation to a consenting adult patient? If terminal sedation becomes a widespread practice with the terminally ill, might it be administered to patients who are not terminally ill? Might the use of terminal sedation smooth society's slide toward active euthanasia?

## Is Terminal Sedation a Form of Killing?

If terminal sedation is not killing, why does it look so much like it? Its clear intention is to hasten a patient's death when sedation is accompanied by the standard practice of withdrawing or withholding food, fluids and other supportive care. Only one conclusion to be drawn from such an act—the death of the patient is intended.

Some argue that the only motive is to relieve pain and suffering for someone whose symptoms cannot be managed in any other way. This is akin to [assisted-suicide proponent] Jack Kevorkian's claim that when he administered carbon monoxide to his "patients" his only intention was to relieve their pain. Likewise, when sedation is accompanied by removal or withholding of all supportive care, the clear outcome will be death.

*"I thought you'd like to know—you've been pencilled in for next Tuesday."*

Rothco. © by Rothco Cartoons, Inc. Reproduced by permission.

Some proponents claim that terminal sedation accompanied by the withholding or withdrawal of supportive care is simply the principle of "double effect" at work. A desired effect (i.e., relief of pain) is achieved while an undesired effect (i.e., hastened death) is also experienced. While appeals to the principle of double effect may carry weight in situations where pain management requires administering increased dosages of medications at the risk of hastening the patient's death through the suppression of respiration, such claims in relation to terminal sedation with hydration/nutrition withdrawal are bogus.

Administering drugs to control pain may increase the risk of a hastened death, albeit an unintended result, however, inducing deep sleep accompanied by ceasing all supportive care leaves the outcome in no doubt. If death is the intended result, then the means by which it is achieved makes no moral difference, regardless of whether the killing is done under medical auspices or not.

## Does Terminal Sedation Undermine the Long-Held Tradition of Hospice?

Due to lingering misconceptions, workers strive continuously to assure patients and families that hospice does not practice euthanasia. The goal of hospice is to give dying patients the highest quality of life for however long they live. While hospice patients have been diagnosed as being terminal, meaning death is expected within one year, this in no way obligates hospice workers to "ensure" that death occurs within this window of time.

Terminal sedation would undermine the core values of hospice by involving hospice personnel in a protocol intended to result in the patient's death—a hastened death. It also sends a not-so-subtle message to other hospice patients that perhaps they, too, should spare their loved ones additional "burdens" and choose a quicker death. While many hospice patients die in their homes, away from other terminal patients, the educational effect of inducing unconsciousness and removal of supportive care undoubtedly spills over to other patients and other families. Furthermore, if terminal sedation is indeed killing, it most definitely violates the care-giving tradition of hospice.

Is the latter charge somewhat mitigated by the nature of the person's suffering? Must we keep a dying person conscious for as long as possible? Do Christian ethical principles require a terminally ill person to remain conscious throughout the dying process? The answer to all of these questions is no. A person is not morally required to consciously experience all of the pain and suffering his or her dying might entail. The appropriate use of pain and sedating medications is, therefore, an acceptable form of comfort care. To make a person permanently unconscious and to withdraw or withhold food and fluids, however, is not comfort care. It is killing, and by definition it violates the care-giving tradition of hospice. For these reasons, the Christian physician may not utilize terminal sedation as an ethically valid form of treatment.

## Terminal Sedation for Nonterminal Patients?

Terminal sedation is not a rarely used last resort, as some proponents claim. Despite the fact that only a few studies on the use of terminal sedation have been conducted, its use runs as high as 52 percent among the terminally ill. When aggravating factors such as cost containment, over-burdened caregivers, and heightened patient awareness of its availability are considered, the incidence of terminal sedation being used for patients experiencing stroke, dementia and other serious illnesses will likely increase.

The precedent has already been set. Living wills and other advance directives have already been used to terminate supportive care for patients who are not imminently dying. If we tolerate just a little bit of deliberate death, albeit with "safeguards," we contribute to the "culture of death." Terminal sedation does not offer patients more control at the end of life. It offers only death.

## Closing Thoughts

Many families reflect fondly on a loved one's final moments. They tell of being blessed to take part in meaningful conversations and to hear their loved one's parting words.

How might terminal sedation alter deathbed scenes? Families would be able to say "good-bye" before the patient is sedated, but the conversation would, in effect, end with the words, "Now we're going to kill you." There is no blessing in that kind of death.

"*U.S. citizens should do everything in their power to convince their federal representatives to . . . approve the medical use of marijuana.*"

# Marijuana Should Be Legalized for Seriously Ill People

Byron Demmer

Marijuana relieves the suffering of seriously ill people, maintains Byron Demmer in the following viewpoint. For this reason, he argues, medical marijuana should be legal in the United States as it is in Canada. Further, argues Demmer, the majority of the American people supports the use of medical marijuana, and by refusing to legalize it the federal government is thwarting the will of the people. Demmer is a freelance writer from Middleport, New York.

As you read, consider the following questions:
1. What is a schedule I substance, as defined by the author?
2. What are some of the therapeutic uses of marijuana, according to Demmer?
3. According to the author, how is Canada's medical marijuana program designed to provide quality, standardized marijuana?

Byron Demmer, "Arrest Suffering, Not Medical Marijuana Patients," *The Humanist*, vol. 61, November/December 2001, p. 35. Copyright © 2001 by the American Humanist Association. Reproduced by permission of the author.

A country that prides itself on freedom and justice should not arrest the seriously ill for using marijuana as a medicine. Common sense and compassion for the suffering of one's fellows dictate that they shouldn't be arrested for seeking relief from their suffering. But they are being arrested in the United States. The federal government continues to enforce federal marijuana laws against medical marijuana users, even in states which have enacted legislation specifically allowing such use. We need to end this injustice by changing the federal law to allow medicinal use of marijuana when recommended by a doctor.

Marijuana was improperly classified by the Federal Controlled Substances Act of 1970 as a schedule I substance—the most restrictive of five categories. A schedule I substance is defined as having a high potential for abuse and no accepted medical use in treatment in the United States. Schedule I substances may not be prescribed by physicians.

## Marijuana Does Have Medicinal Value

Opponents of medical marijuana often support their opposition by claiming a lack of scientific evidence proving its medicinal value. But the nonprofit Washington, D.C.–based Marijuana Policy Project (www.mpp.org) reports there are more than seventy modern studies published in peer-reviewed journals or by government agencies verifying that marijuana does have medicinal value. Moreover, in 1988 the Drug Enforcement Administration's [DEA] own chief administrative law judge, Francis Young, ruled, "Marijuana, in its natural form, is one of the safest therapeutically active substances known. . . . It would be unreasonable, arbitrary, and capricious for DEA to continue to stand between those sufferers and the benefits of this substance."

Marijuana's known therapeutic uses include treatment for relieving chronic pain, relieving nausea, reducing muscle spasms and spasticity, reducing intraocular eye pressure, and increasing appetite. Marijuana can be beneficial to people who suffer from cancer, AIDS, glaucoma, multiple sclerosis, and other ailments.

Recognizing these legitimate medical uses, voters in Alaska,

Arizona, California, Colorado, Hawaii, Maine, Nevada, Oregon, and the state of Washington have already passed legislation allowing its medicinal use. This legislation allows patients to grow, possess, and use medical marijuana when approved by a physician. It permits the assistance of a caregiver who is authorized to help the patient grow, acquire, or consume medical marijuana. And it immunizes physicians from liability for discussing or recommending medical use of marijuana.

The New Mexico governor's office has produced a fact sheet listing organizations which endorse medical access to marijuana. Among them are the Institute of Medicine, the American Academy of Family Physicians, the American Bar Association, the American Public Health Association; the AIDS Action Council, the British Medical Association, the California Medical Association, the California Nurses Association, the California Pharmacists Association, Kaiser Permanente, the National Association of Attorneys General, the New York State Nurses Association, and the *New England Journal of Medicine*.

Support for the medical use of marijuana continues to grow. In Maryland, Donald Murphy (Republican-Catonsville), who is attempting to get a medical marijuana bill passed there,[1] has remarked, "As a state, we have a right and a responsibility to act on behalf of the welfare of our citizens. This only strengthens my resolve to continue fighting for a patient's right to use medical marijuana if it is approved by his or her doctor."

## The Federal Government Is Thwarting the Will of the People

There is also an important constitutional issue embedded in the current medical marijuana debate: namely, where does the federal government get the authority to impose a national policy on the people in the states in question—people who have already elected a contrary policy? Roger Pilon, Ph.D., J.D., a senior fellow and director of the Center for Constitutional Studies of the Cato Institute, raised this point on October 1, 1997, in a statement before the Crime Subcommittee of the Committee on the Judiciary of the U.S. House of

1. The bill did not pass.

## Nationwide Public Opinion Polls on Medical Marijuana

- 80 percent of respondents supported allowing adults to "legally use marijuana for medical purposes."
  POLL: Time Magazine/CNN Poll
  DATE: October 2002
  Sample Size: 1,007

- 70 percent of respondents answered affirmatively to the question, "Should the use of medical marijuana be allowed?"
  POLL: Center for Substance Abuse Research
  DATE: January 2002
  Sample Size: N/A

- 73 percent of respondents supported allowing doctors "to prescribe marijuana."
  POLL: Pew Research Center Poll
  DATE: March 2001
  Sample Size: 1,513

- 73 percent of respondents said they "would vote for making marijuana legally available for doctors to prescribe."
  POLL: Gallup
  DATE: March 1999
  Sample size: 1,018

National Organization for the Reform of Marijuana Laws, 2004.

Representatives. Pilon further observed:

> The Constitution does not establish a national government of general power; rather, it establishes a government of enumerated powers only. . . . There is no federal police power. . . . The police power resides in the individual states—the general governments under our system of dual sovereignty. Thus, regulations to secure rights in the areas of health, safety, and medical practice are the doctrinal and historic province of the states, not the federal government.

However, as a practical matter, as long as the federal laws prohibiting medical marijuana use remain, patients in the states which have legislatively approved its use will be at risk for arrest and imprisonment from federal law enforcement officials. By enforcing a federal law prohibiting possession or use of medical marijuana, the federal government is thwarting the will of the people. Efforts must therefore be made to bring the federal law back in compliance with states' rights and the demonstrated will of the people and to remove the criminal penalties for medical marijuana use.

## Canada Recognizes Marijuana as Medicine

Canada has already done just that. On July 31, 2001, the Marijuana Medical Access Regulations took effect throughout Canada, making it the first country to federally recognize marijuana as a medicine. The Canadian government's Office of Cannabis Medical Access states:

> The regulations establish a compassionate framework to allow the use of marijuana by people who are suffering from serious illnesses, where conventional treatment are inappropriate or are not providing adequate relief of the symptoms related to the medical condition or its treatment, and where the use of marijuana is expected to have some medical benefit that outweighs the risk of its use.

These regulations identify three categories of people who are eligible to possess marijuana for medical purposes:

• those who have a terminal illness and a life expectancy of less than twelve months

• those who suffer from severe pain and/or persistent muscle spasms, cancer, AIDS, severe arthritis, or epilepsy

• those with some other serious medical condition where conventional treatments have failed to provide relief.

To be approved as a participant in this program, an applicant must submit a medical declaration, signed by a physician, that describes the symptom for which marijuana is being prescribed, as well as a specific recommended dosage. Once approved, patients are issued photo identification cards entitling them to grow their own marijuana supply, designate someone else to grow it for them, and obtain it from a Canadian government licensed supplier.

A key part of Canada's medical marijuana program is the use of a government-licensed grower. Prairie Plant Systems, Inc., of Saskatoon, Saskatchewan has been selected as the licensed grower for the Canadian government. According to Health Canada, "The grower will be able to provide a reliable source of affordable, quality, standardized marijuana to meet medical and research needs in Canada."

## Medical Marijuana Should Be Allowed in the United States

In the United States, however, seriously ill people, for whom marijuana is an efficacious and necessary treatment, are faced with a dilemma. Should they obey federal law and suffer unnecessarily, or should they disobey federal law (but not state law in many cases) and use marijuana to ease their suffering? Obviously, placing them in such a position of choice is unfair, and U.S. citizens should do everything in their power to convince their federal representatives to correct this situation and approve the medical use of marijuana.

*"At present, the evidence in favor of marijuana's utility as a medicine remains anecdotal and unproven."*

# Marijuana Should Not Be Legalized for Seriously Ill People

Part I: Mark Souder; Part II: Janet M. LaRue

In the following two-part viewpoint, both Mark Souder and Janet M. LaRue argue that legalization of marijuana for medical use is unnecessary and would be harmful to society. There is no proof that marijuana is an effective medicine for the seriously ill, they state, and legalization would have negative consequences, such as increased illegal drug use among the general population. In addition, they point out, more effective marijuana derivatives are available for the seriously ill. Souder is a U.S. congressman from Indiana. LaRue is senior director of legal studies at the Family Research Council, a nonprofit organization that provides information and policy research about issues affecting the United States.

As you read, consider the following questions:
1. According to the 1999 Institute of Medicine study cited by Souder, what is the only possible future for marijuana as a medicine?
2. How does LaRue refute the claim that marijuana has helped control aspects of various diseases?
3. What have been the negative consequences of past periods of marijuana legalization, according to LaRue?

Part I: Mark Souder, testimony before the U.S. House Subcommittee on Criminal Justice, Drug Policy and Human Resources, Committee on Government Reform, Washington, DC, April 1, 2004. Part II: Janet M. LaRue, "Do State Laws Allowing for the Medical Use of Marijuana Violate Federal Drug Laws?" *Supreme Court Debates*, May 2001.

# I

In recent years, a large and well-funded pro-drug movement has succeeded in convincing many Americans that marijuana is a true medicine to be used in treating a wide variety of illnesses. Unable to change the federal laws, however, these pro-drug activists turned to the state referendum process and succeeded in passing a number of medical marijuana initiatives.

This has set up a direct conflict between federal and state law, and put into sharp focus the competing scientific claims —about the value of marijuana and its components as medicine.

## Anecdotal Evidence

Marijuana was once used as a folk remedy in many primitive cultures, and even in the 19th century was frequently used by some American doctors, much as alcohol, cocaine and heroin were once also used by doctors.

By the 20th century, however, its use by legitimate medical practitioners had dwindled, while its illegitimate use as a recreational drug had risen.

The drug was finally banned as a medicine in the 1930s. Beginning in the 1970s, however, individuals began reporting anecdotal evidence that marijuana might have medically beneficial uses, most notably in suppressing the nausea associated with cancer chemotherapy.

Today, the evidence is still essentially anecdotal, but many people take it as a fact that marijuana is a proven medicine. At present, the evidence in favor of marijuana's utility as a medicine remains anecdotal and unproven. . . .

## Negative Effects

In contrast to its supposed medical benefits, the negative health effects of marijuana are well known and have been proven in scientific studies. Among other things, the drug is addictive, impairs brain function, and when smoked greatly, increases the risk of lung cancer.

The respiratory problems associated with smoking any substance makes the use of marijuana cigarettes as medicine highly problematic. Indeed, no modern medicine is smoked.

It is quite possible, however, that some components of marijuana may have legitimate medical uses. Indeed, [a 1999] Institute of Medicine report, so often erroneously cited as supporting smoked marijuana, actually stated that, quote, "If there is any future of marijuana as a medicine, it lies in its isolated components, the cannabinoids, and their synthetic derivatives."

Interestingly, the federal government has already approved a marijuana derivative called Marinol, but rarely do the pro-marijuana advocates mention this.

# II

[Legalizing medical marijuana] is unnecessary and the harm will outweigh any benefits. The principal active ingredient in marijuana, delta-9-tetrahydrocannabinol (THC), is available in a prescribable pill called Marinol; it is also available as a rectal suppository that allows patients to absorb THC faster than Marinol or smoking crude marijuana.

THC, however, is a mind-altering and dangerous substance. THC affects cognition, memory, pain perception, and motor coordination. It produces euphoria and relaxation but also can deliver anxiety and panic reactions. The user's heart rate is severely elevated for up to three hours.

Crude marijuana is bad medicine that harms the brain, heart, and lungs; it limits learning, memory, perception, judgment, and complex motor skills. While the evidence supports the selective use of pure THC to treat nausea associated with cancer chemotherapy and to stimulate appetite, the evidence does not support the reclassification (to Schedule II, a prescribable drug) of crude marijuana.[1] The delivery system is unhealthful and unreliable.

Marijuana smoke increases the risks for cancer, lung damage, and problems with pregnancies, including low birth weight. In addition, plants contain a variable mixture of biologically active compounds and cannot be expected to provide a precisely defined drug effect.

Pro-marijuana arguments heavily rely on anecdotal evi-

---

1. Marijuana is currently classified as a Schedule I substance, which may not be prescribed by a physician and has no accepted medical use in the United States.

# Result of Legalization Initiatives

A new Arizona survey finds that more adolescents in Arizona use drugs, compared to their national counterparts.

Since 1996, Arizona voters have passed several ballot initiatives that have moved the state towards [marijuana] legalization. . . . Laws that appear to condone drug use and perceived availability of drugs are two risk factors for increased drug use by young people, according to [researchers] David Hawkins and Richard Catalano. The [2002] Arizona survey appears to confirm their findings.

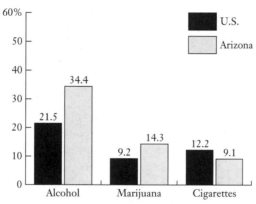

**Past-Month Drug Use**
Arizona 8th Graders vs. U.S. 8th Graders

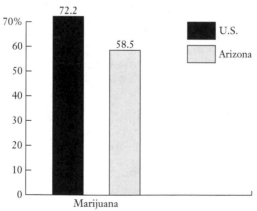

**Perception of Harm**
Arizona 8th Graders vs. U.S. 8th Graders

National Families in Action, 2002.

dence instead of controlled studies. Many people make the claim that marijuana use has helped control aspects of various diseases. Marijuana is addictive and addicts tend to feel better when they receive their drug.

## Legalization Would Have a Negative Impact on Society

Permitting "medicalization" of crude marijuana would result in many negative consequences that the Federal drug laws are designed to prevent. Medicalization changes society's (particularly children's) attitudes toward the perceived dangerousness of illicit drug use.

There is a high correlation between marijuana use and many social and public health harms. Studies find that a high percentage of reckless drivers and accident victims used marijuana. A study testing urine samples of reckless drivers who were not obviously drunk from alcohol found that 59 percent of the drivers tested positive for cocaine and marijuana.

Past periods of legalization of marijuana have produced negative consequences. Dutch tolerance of drug use has created a climate that drug manufacturers and traffickers have seized upon to produce and market more addictive and dangerous drugs. This has led to the Netherlands becoming a major producer of illicit synthetic drugs.

Medicalization of marijuana is a pretense used by many advocates of legalization. An April 1999 article in *Proceedings of the Association of American Physicians* states, "Most supporters of smoked marijuana are hostile to the use of purified chemicals from marijuana, insisting that only smoked marijuana leaves be used as 'medicine,' revealing clearly that their motivation is not scientific medicine but the back-door legalization of marijuana." In 1999, Barry McCaffrey, director of the Office of National Drug Control Policy, warned a congressional committee of "a carefully camouflaged, well-funded, tightly knit core of people whose goal is to legalize drug use in the United States."

# Periodical Bibliography

The following articles have been selected to supplement the diverse views presented in this chapter.

| | |
|---|---|
| *American Medical News* | "Physician-Assisted Suicide: When Pain Trails Other Concerns," March 19, 2001. |
| William Buckley | "Does Marijuana Help Sick People?" *Conservative Chronicle*, November 6, 2002. |
| Alexander Cockburn | "The Right Not to Be in Pain," *Nation*, February 3, 2003. |
| William S. Eidelman and Eric A. Voth | "Should Physicians Support the Use of Medical Marijuana?" *Western Journal of Medicine*, March 2002. |
| August Gribbin | "A Graceful Exit," *Washington Times*, January 7, 2001. |
| Bill Keller | "Reefer Madness: Pot Is Not the Problem, or the Solution," *New York Times*, November 30, 2002. |
| Billy R. Martin | "Medical Marijuana: Moving Beyond the Smoke," *Lancet*, July 6, 2002. |
| Judith McFarland | "In the Eye of the Beholder," *Nursing*, June 2002. |
| Ron Panzer | "Terminal Sedation: Good Palliative Care or Euthanasia?" *Hospice Patients Alliance Newsletter*, September 16, 2002. |
| David Sharp | "Highs and Lows of Canabis," *Lancet*, January 31, 2004. |
| David Tuller | "Doctors Tread a Thin Line on Marijuana Advice," *New York Times*, October 28, 2003. |
| Nancy Valko | "Sedated to Death?: When 'Comfort Care' Becomes Dangerous," www.lifeissues.net, 2002. |
| Amy Villet-Lagomarsino | "The Double Effect: Terminal Sedation," www.pbs.org, 2000. |

# CHAPTER 3

# How Can the Spiritual and Emotional Pain of Terminal Illness Be Eased?

# Chapter Preface

In a 1997 issue of *Common Boundary* magazine, columnist Pythia Peay relates the story of her father's death. According to Peay, she had imagined that the approaching death would mirror her father's life, in which he was emotionally isolated from, and in conflict with, other family members. "I steeled myself for the worst," she admits, But then "a miracle happened—in fact, a host of them." Peay describes how her father let his death become a time of growth, and how because of this, his death experience became a good one. "When my father died, he was at home surrounded by a loving family," she says. "He had made his peace with estranged relatives and God. He had completed a will, reconciled with the Church, and even helped plan a funeral. . . . His dying became a kind of party—sending out for his favorite foods, socializing with family, enjoying a few last drinks and cigarettes."

Like Peay, there are many people who believe that the pain of death can be substantially eased if the terminally ill embrace the end of life as a time of growth. Buddhist teacher Christine Longaker maintains that people's lives consist of a number of stages of growth, which includes dying. According to her, "Dying becomes another stage of living, a very vital stage that can allow us to conclude our lives well." Writer Connie McPeak Green echoes Longaker with her suggestion that the terminally ill should view their final days as a "time of sacred transformation." She believes that the dying should see their last days as a precious time in which to accomplish those things that they did not accomplish in their lives. "During our dying we have one last opportunity to become the person we had hoped to be," she points out. "We have the opportunity to ask for forgiveness and to forgive both ourselves and others."

However, not everyone takes such a positive view of dying. Professor Marshall B. Kapp rejects the idea that the end of life should be a time of growth and acceptance. In his opinion, viewing death this way will not ease the pain of dying. "There are still a few of us left who think that dying . . . stinks, and that there really is no effective way to do it well," he states. Kapp explains what his reaction to dying would be:

"My reaction to the bad news would be one of anger, frustration, terror, and bitter feelings of injustice," he says. "And . . . these sentiments would intensify rather than mellow as the dying process proceeded. I might not want to tell those with whom I had conflicts that, in the end, I forgive and love them." In Kapp's opinion, the dying have no obligation to make up for past mistakes, and should have the right to "die mad, with a frown instead of a smile."

As the debate over growth at the end of life illustrates, the terminally ill experience severe spiritual and emotional pain. There is continued disagreement over whether that pain can be eased, and how to do so. The authors in the following chapter offer several insights on this controversial topic.

|"First and foremost, dying patients want
their physicians to talk to them and their
families openly."

# Doctors Should Speak Openly with Patients and Their Families About Death

Kerri Wachter

Most doctors have difficulty speaking openly with terminally ill patients and their families, maintains Kerri Wachter
in the following viewpoint. According to Wachter, doctors
frequently try to insulate themselves with distancing tactics.
Instead, she argues, they should learn to speak more openly
with both patients and their families about illness and death.
Wachter is a senior writer for *Family Practice News*, an independent newspaper that provides news and commentary
about developments in health care.

As you read, consider the following questions:

1. What type of distancing tactics do physicians commonly
use, according to the author?
2. Why do terminal patients tend to feel that their
physicians are abandoning them, as cited by Wachter?
3. In the author's opinion, how does explaining the death
process help patients and their families?

Kerri Wachter, "End-of-Life Care Takes Compassion and Finesse: Involvement
Doesn't Stop at Diagnosis," *Family Practice News*, vol. 33, November 1, 2003,
p. 33. Copyright © 2003 by the International Medical News Group. Reproduced
by permission.

When the 43-year-old man checked into the hospital with severe stomach pain, 2 months later it wasn't his doctor who told him and his family that he was dying. It was a palliative care consultant they had not met before.

"When I talked with the family they told me that they hadn't talked with the doctor. They didn't know anything except that this relative was terribly ill," said Dr. John P. McNulty of the Palliative Care Institute of Southeast Louisiana, Covington. "They were quite upset that things were this bad, and they had not been included."

The man died that day. "This really left a bad taste in my mouth," Dr. McNulty said at the annual meeting of the American Academy of Family Physicians.

For a variety of reasons, physicians don't always do such a great job of caring for terminal patients. Dealing with death in general is difficult; dealing with the coming death of a patient is even more difficult; said Dr. Steve Taylor, Hospice of St. Tammany, Covington.

## Physicians Can Help Improve the Dying Process

Without realizing it, physicians sometimes rely on distancing tactics to insulate themselves. "We use some very sophisticated, subtle defense mechanisms rather than face—in our eyes—the failure of death," Dr. Taylor said. Some physicians give premature or false reassurances, normalize the situation, pay selective attention, "jolly" along, pass the buck, turn a deaf ear, concentrate on physical tasks, or disappear altogether.

But patients don't see terminal illness as the physician's failure. "They don't expect us to have the answers about death. They expect us to have the answers about pneumonia and what foods to eat, but nobody expects us to have the answers about death," Dr. Taylor said.

"I like to think of our position as the coach of a losing team. A losing team can be held together by the coach or they can fragment and start to point fingers at each other. It's our job to prepare them for that last journey," he said.

Over the last few years, Dr. McNulty has talked with many dying patients and their families about their needs and how physicians can improve care during the dying process. The same themes came up over and over.

First and foremost, dying patients want their physicians to talk to them and their families openly. "Often we throw up barriers. We have time constraints or we're not trained to be comfortable talking with these patients and their families. But it's so terribly important."

---

## Preparing for Death

Claudia West is dealing with the one certainty she's found in an unpredictable illness: She's dying.

West, 47, has multiple sclerosis in a form that's burning through her quickly. Diagnosed just four years ago in [1998], she's now nearly bedbound, in hospice care.

When doctors told her she was dying, she felt liberated, she says. Now, she and her husband, Rick, and their children can talk about what's happening to her body in ways they couldn't before. No one's saying "Don't even think such a thing" about her eventual death. She's done paperwork and had crucial conversations with people she adores, including the father to whom she was not close growing up.

She even summoned up the strength to make a tiny angel quilt, which hangs over the bed in her room. She carefully stitched the bright fabric, adding a whimsical fluff of synthetic hair, shortly after her doctors told her she was dying. It's a way for her to tell her daughters that she's changing worlds soon but will continue to love and, she believes, watch over them.

Care changes when focus shifts from seeking a cure to acknowledging death's proximity. Much of the change, says West, is for the better.

Lois M. Collins and Elaine Jarvik, *Deseret Morning News*, August 29, 2002.

---

Keep the lines of communication simple. Patients or families shouldn't have to go through several people to get answers.

It's important to be aware of cultural differences as well. All cultures have developed their own customs surrounding death and it's important to respect these.

## Breaking the News

Breaking the news of a terminal illness can be the hardest thing that physicians will have to do, but more than 90% of patients want to know if they have a terminal illness, Dr. McNulty said. He recommended the following process of breaking this news to patients:

- Set the stage by finding a quiet private place, where you won't be disturbed.
- Acknowledge everyone in the room and ask their relationship to the patient; maintain eye contact.
- Ask the patient and the family what they already know.
- Find out how much they want to know.
- Give them the news, pause, and wait for a reaction.
- Establish a plan of action.
- Answer their questions.
- Pledge your support.

Let them know that you will be there. "It's important for the patient and family to know that you're there as their advocate," he said.

Terminal patients tend to feel that their physicians and medicine in general are abandoning them. "This phrase 'There's nothing more than we can do'—there's got to be a better way to say that," Dr. McNulty said. For the patients, that phrase connotes that the physician is abandoning them and moving on to the next case. Patients in this situation feel very vulnerable and need to know that they have someone they can trust.

## Preparing for the End

Dr. McNulty also said that patients tell him that they want their wishes to be respected. To this end, it's important for a patient to have a set of advance directives, though he notes that it's difficult to get patients to think about this.

It's important to teach patients and family what to expect, Dr. Taylor said. "In hospice, the more we tell people what to expect—no matter what it is—they feel better if they know." Explaining the death process helps to reduce fear by reducing pain and suffering, it improves compliance, and it removes the intolerable uncertainty.

This is also a time for healing relationships with family and friends, he said. There are four things that you need to tell your patients to say to those who are close to them: You are important to me. Please forgive me. I forgive you. Goodbye.

Lastly patients want someone to help relieve their suffering, Dr. McNulty said. It's often easy enough to relieve physical pain, but remember that there are all kinds of pain—

physical, psychological, emotional, and spiritual.

Spirituality is a subject that makes some physicians uneasy, Dr. Taylor said. It doesn't matter what the physicians believes; what matters is what the patient believes. He recommended asking patients about FICA: faith, importance, community, and address. Ask them what they believe in, how important it is to them, whether they have a community of faith that they want to involve in their dying process, and how they want you as their physicians to address their spirituality.

To better understand the stages of dying, Dr. Taylor recommends "On Death and Dying" by Dr. Elisabeth Kübler-Ross (New York: Scribner Classics, 1997).

*"Only in facing our deaths can we fully experience the preciousness of our lives."*

# Embracing Feelings About Death Before Becoming Ill Is Beneficial

Fred Branfman

Most people do not spend much time thinking about the fact that they will eventually die, asserts Fred Branfman in the following viewpoint. However, he argues, it is important to face that fact before terminal illness or death strikes. Embracing the idea of death is a good way to prepare for it, says Branfman, and it helps ensure that the death experience will be a good one. Branfman is a freelance writer living in Santa Barbara, California.

As you read, consider the following questions:

1. According to Branfman, who inspired the "death and dying movement"?
2. What does the author believe is one of the last taboos in twenty-first century America?
3. In Bruce Bendinger's opinion, why have the majority of baby boomers failed to think about death?

As the candle burns brightest in the darkness, so too is life most fully lived with a day-to-day awareness of death. We spend much of our lives seeking happiness, satisfaction and meaning, imagining that they can best be found by ignoring our feelings about our own mortality. But there is a surprising amount of evidence, including new books by Studs Terkel and Virginia Morris, that few experiences can confer a greater sense of the preciousness of life, profound love, compassion and a sense of the spiritual than openly engaging our feelings about that fact that we will one day die. It is not easy to do so. But we may discover our full potential for life only if we are also willing to face our anguish about its ending.

## Death Anxiety

Much progress has been made, of course, on bringing death out of the closet. There is even a "death and dying" movement, inspired by Dr. Elisabeth Kübler-Ross, devoted to helping people die as painlessly as possible and to counseling their loved ones. But it is still revolutionary to suggest that people in the prime of life might benefit from surfacing and working with long-repressed feelings about their eventual demise. Discussing how death anxiety influences how we live is perhaps the last taboo in a 21st century America that has put virtually every other issue—from AIDS to Viagra—on the table.

We all know intellectually that we will die, of course. But we tend to avoid thinking about it, and to feel our feelings about it even less. As Angelina Rossi, the mother of a Vietnam vet and a Terkel interviewee, put it: "I find that the majority of people don't want to discuss death. It happens to everyone else, but it's not going to happen to us." This formulation recalls the classic Indian story, the Mahabharata. Yudhishthira, the hero, is asked by Yama, the god of death, "what is the most wondrous thing you know about human beings?" "That all humans, though seeing death all around them, think they will live forever," he answers.

Ernest Becker's classic, "The Denial of Death," powerfully explained how we repress our feelings about our own mortality. We first learn as youngsters between the ages of 3 and 8 that we will die. But we deny the feelings this knowledge evokes because we do not have the emotional tools to cope with them. We then unconsciously take this mode of death denial into our adult lives, rarely examining whether it is really in our interests to do so.

## Denial Is Harmful

If a wide variety of existential psychologists and thinkers are right, however, we lead far more deadened lives than we realize when we deny our deepest feelings about death. We devote much psychic energy to death-denial, reducing our aliveness. We cut off feelings for loved ones out of an unconscious fear of losing them. Unconsciously wishing to live on through our children, we often punish them when they do not turn out as we wish. Turning religion or nationalism into projects to achieve immortality often leads to violent consequences, as we have just so tragically witnessed.

Denial of death also robs us of the positive value of engaging our feelings about our mortality. As Terkel notes: "We, as a matter of course, reflect on death, voice hope and fear, only when a dear one is near death, or out of it. Why not speak of it while we're in the flower of good health? How can we envision our life, the one we now experience, unless we recognize that it is finite?"

Of the 61 people Terkel interviewed, Maurine Young's story is perhaps the most striking. Her 19-year-old son Andrew was killed by 18-year-old gang member Mario Ramos. Young describes how she moved from wanting to see her son's killer executed to forgiving him, culminating in an emotional jail cell meeting. "I love you like you're my son, like you're one of mine. . . . You got into my heart violently, but you're there," she told him.

She explained that facing death led to deep love: "It really took the murder of my son and the forgiving of his killer to teach me how to forgive everybody around me. By forgiving them, like I did Mario, it freed me to really love."

## No Reason to Fear Death

Others were similarly transformed by facing death. Dr. John Barrett's daily exposure to death made him worry less about the trivial things in life like his car breaking down. Filmmaker

Haskell Wexler spoke of how being in his late 70s has led him to value personal relations more than his work. Comedian Mick Betancourt said that becoming aware of life's brevity has led him to take greater risks with his career. Most of Terkel's interviewees also report that they do not fear death. Many base this on deep religious or spiritual beliefs that convince them that death is not the end. Even a nonbeliever like Kurt Vonnegut Jr. takes a matter-of-fact attitude: "In [my novel] 'Slaughterhouse-Five,' every time somebody dies . . . I always say: 'So it goes'—that's all. Whenever anybody had died—and this would be my sister, my brother, my father, my mother, and I was nearby for those events—that's how I felt. . . ."

## Difficulty of Talking About Death

In any family, talking about death is likely to be emotionally loaded. Simply raising the topic brings with it an acknowledgement that someone is not going to live forever, that someone will die before someone else, and that there will be grief and mourning by survivors, whatever form it may take.

In addition, there is always family history about what death is, what it represents, and what death has done to family members, including survivors. There can be histories of family members who died at a young age, who died in a war, who died from painful diseases, who were murdered, who never knew their mother or father, or whose lives were shattered by a death of a beloved family member.

Furthermore, there are family traditions that may stick in people's minds, such as having had to kiss a grandparent in the coffin, going to loud and raucous wakes, watching a parent cry or never cry, never being told that a parent has died, or being able to go to a family funeral because one was "too young."

Mark Edinberg, www.ec-online.net, 2000.

Morris, whose important new book is a wake-up call on the need to approach death consciously, does not understand such views. "I'm always surprised when people tell me they are not afraid of dying. My guess is that most people who say this simply have not given the subject enough thought, for fear of death, as far as I can tell, comes with being human," she writes.

Morris makes the strong case that the end of life can be

one of our most beautiful experience, if we prepare for it. If not, it can be agonizing. "We must not wait because by the time we determine that we are 'there,' at that magical border, we have quite often, missed our chance," she writes.

Her book is painful to read. At times I felt like throwing it across the room, as it forced me to confront the inevitability of the fates awaiting my loved ones and myself. But in the end I had to admit that I owe it to them and myself to face my death as squarely as I can.

The reader of Terkel's book is left to wonder whether his reports of people who say they do not fear death represent wisdom or denial. He might have probed more deeply, for example, whether they are preparing for the death of their loved ones and themselves, as Morris recommends.

## The Need to Slow Down

Such questions are important not only for each of us as individuals, but for society as a whole. Seventy-seven-million baby boomers will die in the coming decades. This generation exhibited an unusual capacity for self-reflection in its youth, producing the sexual, women's, gay and environmental revolutions. If it turns its attention to consciously living out of its last years with an enhanced awareness of its mortality and the legacy it is leaving, the world and future generations could be far better off.

Doing so will require a major shift from present boomer consciousness, however. In one of Terkel's more insightful interviews, advertising guru Bruce Bendinger says, "I was born during World War II, a baby boomer. We've had our foot on the gas for fifty years. And now, as we hit the twenty-first century, we have really accelerated past what is good for people. You're not really thinking. So how can we think about such a thing as death?"

Indeed. Whether baby boomers are able to slow down and savor what is genuinely important in life may determine not only their own happiness in their remaining years, but the quality of society and the legacy they will leave.

People who feel their deepest emotions about their own mortality often report an enhanced appreciation of life, including more compassion for those different from themselves, a greater concern for nature and the environment, less concern for material possessions, more spiritual openings and greater generosity.

Future generations' lives will depend upon our mercy. Whether they will remember us well may depend upon our heeding Terkel's call. Only in facing our deaths can we fully experience the preciousness of our lives.

> *"Doctors who miss the experience of the human spirit are like readers who skip several chapters in a book: they do not truly comprehend the whole."*

# Doctors Should Address the Spirituality of the Terminally Ill

Myles N. Sheehan

*In the following viewpoint Myles N. Sheehan argues that an important part of end-of-life care is attention to spirituality. In Sheehan's opinion, by addressing the spiritual needs of their patients doctors can better understand them, make more appropriate treatment decisions, and ease the dying process. This type of care, he argues, is just as important as high-technology treatments. Sheehan is senior associate dean at the Stritch School of Medicine, Loyola University Medical Center, Chicago.*

As you read, consider the following questions:

1. What is the difference between religion and spirituality, as argued by Sheehan?
2. How is being a good doctor like being a good reader, in the author's opinion?
3. According to the author, why is it beneficial to allow a patient to express spiritual pain?

Myles N. Sheehan, "Spirituality and Care at the End of Life," www.partnership forcaring.org, September 2000. Originally appeared in *Choice in Dying News*, vol. 6, no. 4, Summer 1997. This version updated in 2000 by Partnership for Caring. Reproduced by permission of the author.

What does it mean to attend to the spiritual needs of patients as they face serious illness? And what, if any, impact does a person's spirituality have on choices at the end of life? Does the openness of caregivers to a patient's spiritual experience affect their interaction with patients? Could explicit attention to spirituality help doctors and patients be frank about the goals of treatment and a person's choices about therapy?

## The Definition of Spirituality

Spirituality may conjure up a variety of images, some not at all flattering, and further definition is required. Philosophers, cognitive psychologists and theologians have speculated endlessly about what it means to be human and about the nature and the interaction of body, mind and spirit. Despite the complexity of the arguments, we humans are both body and spirit; we face life in ways that are more than physical reactions; and our understanding of what it means to be human includes a dimension that both encompasses and goes beyond our physicality. There are at least three components to this spiritual dimension. First, spirituality is an expression of how a person relates to a larger whole, be it God, a higher power or the human family. Second, personal spirituality provides a source of meaning and understanding about the significance of being human. Third, personal spirituality often contains habits, rituals, gestures and symbols that can help a person interpret and manage existence.

Some physicians and others become quite nervous during any discussion of spirituality in medicine. They might fear that spirituality means enforcing particular religious beliefs. However, spirituality and religion are not synonymous. Religious belief is one very important way in which many people express their spirituality. But a person can be spiritual without explicit religious belief. Individuals have a variety of ways to find meaning in life; people come to an understanding of their choices and behaviors. And it is not uncommon to discover that a poem, or a piece of music or a good meal in the company of friends can provide a context through which one can grow and endure, or even accept diminishment. Personal spirituality frequently is expressed by forms of religious practice. Faith provides a variety of personal and communal resources to handle serious illness. Serious illness causes believers and nonbelievers alike to face loss, fears, grief, personal mortality and questions of meaning. These are issues that appropriately are identified, at least partially, as spiritual.

## Physicians and Spirituality

Why should doctors bother with spirituality? Three reasons are readily apparent. First, a doctor who inquires about a patient's spirituality gains a deeper insight into the patient's experience. Being a good doctor can be a bit like being a good reader. Doctors see, touch, hear and participate in some of the most visceral parts of the human experience: birth, death, illness, recovery. They confront and can share in their patient's emotions of hope, despair, joy and profound sorrow. Physicians look through the chapters in a person's life to access a story that contains both the mundane and the extraordinary. Doctors who miss the experience of the human spirit are like readers who skip several chapters in a book: they do not truly comprehend the whole because they avoided crucial information.

Second, knowing all the chapters of a patient's story and gaining insight into the person's spiritual journey can provide a context for making medical decisions. As a person faces the end of life, the context can be especially crucial. For all the discussion and interest in informed consent, advance directives and patients' rights, attempts to care for individuals at the end of life often are filled with poor communication and with the inappropriate use of technology. This might well reflect the inability of doctors and patients to speak the same language. Doctors ask about ventilators, CPR, intubation, feeding tubes. Patients and families talk about death with dignity, refusing to give up, hopes for miracles, requests to be left alone. If a physician understands a person's spiritual response to illness, better communication might result. Two examples might help illustrate the point. A person frightened about death, concerned about what will happen to a spouse and children, and despairing at the loss of hopes and dreams might cling to illusory hope about technology, or focus on the possible life-prolonging aspect of a particular therapy. The result could be an extensive period of aggressive care, the end result of which is increased suffering and death. A doctor who can ask about fears, hopes and despair might find the tools to ease spiritual pain without blindly resorting to invasive treatments that will not bring the patient the peace he or she seeks. Likewise, an individual who has come to the end of an illness can communicate to a physician spiritual acceptance of mortality. The doctor is in a better position to discuss care that is compatible with the person's view of the dying process.

## What Is Important at the End of Life

When I am dying, I am quite sure that the central issues for me will not be whether I am put on ventilator, whether CPR is attempted when my heart stops, or whether I receive artificial feeding. Although each of these could be important, each will almost certainly be quite peripheral. Rather, my central concerns will be how to face my death, how to bring my life to a close, and how best to help my family go on without me. A ventilator will not help me do these things—not unless all I need is a little more time to get the job done.

Unfortunately, however, bioethics has succumbed to the agendas of physicians. Physicians face ethical concerns about treatment decisions—when to offer, withhold, and withdraw various treatments—and treatment decisions have been the focus of bioethics as well. But the issues that most trouble patients and their families at the end of life are not these. To them, the end of life is a spiritual crisis. . . .

Facing death brings to the surface questions about what life is all about. Long-buried assumptions and commitments are revealed. And many find that the beliefs and values they have lived by no longer seem valid or do not sustain them. These are the ingredients of a spiritual crisis, the stuff of spiritual suffering. . . .

Thus perhaps many requests for futile treatment reflect the fact that patients and their families have not completed the essential human tasks of dying.

John Hardwig, *Hastings Center Report*, March 2000.

A third reason doctors should be concerned about a patient's spiritual experience is that it can allow doctors to help patients in a way that is fundamental to medicine: limiting suffering and not abandoning patients to the experience of illness. As people die, they could be in a spiritual distress as deep as any physical pain. Allowing a patient to express spiritual pain is one way to help heal a person's spirit, especially when physical cure is impossible. Helping a patient find spiritual resources and assistance is another way of providing care. Arranging a meeting with a chaplain, facilitating a call to clergy or allowing the patient and family to pray and conduct devotions in a hospital environment can succor a patient at the end of life. An awareness of and respect for common religious practices around death and dying are integral to compassionate care for terminally ill patients. Ritual and prayer are important vehicles by which the human spirit finds meaning in and transcends grief, pain and loss. For example, a doctor who does not know how to show respect for the body of an Orthodox Jew at the time of death or who is ignorant about the significance and power of the Sacrament of the Sick for Roman Catholics lacks key ways to diminish the spiritual suffering of patients and families.

How do doctors and other caregivers access their patients' spirituality? Three simple suggestions provide a starting point. One, do not avoid the subject if patients discuss questions of meaning or their need for specific religious practices. Two, ask simple questions: Can you help me understand what it has been like for you to be sick? What have you found hardest to cope with? What are your sources of strength? What keeps you going? Is God or religion important to you as you face your illness? Three, willingly help patients and families find spiritual resources if they so desire.

## Obstacles

Obstacles and problems occur in integrating spirituality with medicine. Physicians might be reluctant to get involved with questions that make them uncomfortable and that they have failed to address personally, although it is unlikely that a doctor who has not confronted the possibility of personal illness and death would be good at caring for very ill people. Second, a profound ignorance about spirituality and religion exists in America. Because of this ignorance, some will seek to find a conflict between the scientific practice of medicine and topics like spirituality and religion. Neither belief in the human spirit nor faith in God implies antipathy toward science or advocacy of nontraditional medicine. Third, some sensationalize the topic of spirituality in medicine, suggesting a lunatic fringe appeal. The media often focus on spectacular claims of faith healing, alleged miracles and extraordinary experiences, rather than on a doctor's simple concern about his patient's response to illness, fears, hopes and source of meaning in life and death. Obstacles and problems aside, however, recognizing the spiritual side of illness opens up new dimensions for caring.

## Rediscovery

Is there anything particularly new about spirituality in medicine? Probably not. It is more a rediscovery of something that once was taken for granted. Before doctors had much in the way of technology, they knew how to attend their patients even when little could be done in the face of disease or serious illness. Now that doctors have a variety of ways to care for people, including life-saving and life-prolonging high-technology treatments, we must rediscover ways to care for the human spirit.

*"Generations of physicians have earned—indeed prided themselves on—their reputation as stoic technicians. But today's doctors . . . don't have to wall in their emotions."*

# Doctors Should Show More Compassion Toward the Terminally Ill

Rachel K. Sobel

In the following viewpoint Rachel K. Sobel argues that in addition to providing medical treatment for the dying, doctors also need to practice compassion. Medication is not enough to ease the pain of the terminally ill, asserts Sobel. She believes that only by speaking openly with their patients about death and by listening to their fears can doctors help ensure that the death experience is peaceful and dignified. Sobel is an associate editor at *U.S. News & World Report*. She has written numerous articles about science and health issues.

As you read, consider the following questions:
1. In Sobel's opinion, why do terminally ill patients need to receive explicit information about their illness?
2. What important skill do many physicians lack, in the author's opinion?
3. According to Sobel, what might ease the pain of the terminally ill more than futile medications?

Rachel K. Sobel, "The Time Before Dying," *U.S. News & World Report*, vol. 136, April 19, 2004, p. 74.

From the doctor's viewpoint, he had exhausted all treatment options and that was the end of it. Yet the patient, who was dying of cancer, asked if he might continue to come in every week anyway, since he found the visits comforting. But the doctor felt he had nothing left to give him, and turned him away.

This true story is told and retold at the University of California–San Francisco [UCSF], where I am a second-year med student. Our professor, who shared the vignette recently, did so to illustrate a sadly missed opportunity in medicine. The physician may have used all of his cancer expertise, but he failed to use all of his compassion.

## New Focus on Helping the Dying

This lesson was part of a new addition to our curriculum on end-of-life care. Just a decade ago, students at UCSF had one or two lectures at most on the topic. "It was a really big hole, both nationally and locally," says William Shore, a UCSF family medicine professor who helped design the course. We now have more than a dozen hours of required training in palliative care. We attend lectures and discussions on such topics as "Care of Dying Patients and Their Families" and "Breaking Bad News." Residents share their memories of the first patient death they witnessed. And we visit hospices, talk to chaplains, and shadow palliative-care specialists. The result is a much deeper appreciation, early on in medical school, of how physicians can help dying patients.

I visited a 92-year-old patient this winter [2003] as part of this curriculum. He lay comfortably in a twin-size bed and had photographs on the wall: a recent family reunion, a close-up of him sharing a laugh with his late wife. He reminisced about his life as a political activist in New York and his volunteer work for the McGovern campaign. And he loved to talk about his kids. One was a Peace Corps worker in Ukraine. Another edited a small newspaper.

Had I not been at the Coming Home Hospice, I wouldn't have even known this man was dying. He had a rare blood disease, and his doctor had given him a month to live. But this patient taught me that dying could be peaceful and dignified. There were no tubes invading his body. He suffered no pain. "The staff takes very good care of me here," he said.

The new coursework has taught us to talk openly with patients, not to skirt difficult issues. Studies show that despite doctors' fears about dashing hopes, patients indeed want to talk about illness and death when it is approaching. Explicit information enables them to plan better—not just financially but emotionally as well. However, these sensibilities don't come naturally. At UCSF, we are actively working to cultivate such openness. In small groups, we recently tackled a tough assignment: Reflect and write for 10 minutes about death. Then, discuss.

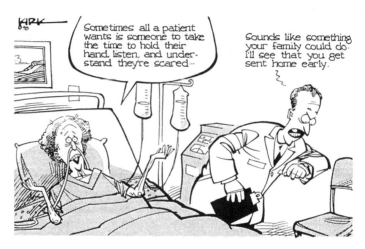

Kirk. © 1998 by Kirk Anderson. Reproduced by permission.

The professor in our group went first. Tears welled up in her eyes as she recalled her father's recent death and her feeling of being alone in the world, an adult but orphaned just the same. We passed the tissue box around—a sudden death of a cousin, a mourned grandparent.

It was for me one of the more daunting assignments in medical school. But it was also one of the most illuminating. Generations of physicians have earned—indeed prided themselves on—their reputation as stoic technicians. But today's doctors, or at least aspiring doctors, don't have to wall in their emotions.

## Lessons for Life

Listening, we're learning, can be a potent tool in dealing with these touchy issues. What do you hope for? What worries you most? Whom can you turn to for support? It sounds simple, but, unfortunately, physicians often lack good listening skills. One study found that residents who were discussing do-not-resuscitate orders with patients talked nearly 80 percent of the time.

Close listening might reveal that some patients' greatest existential fear is not of dying but of never having lived at all. Encourage them, our professors say, to tell stories. Instead of more futile medications, prescribe writing a journal or assembling a photographic tour of the past. Maybe dying patients will be inspired to compose a memoir—or in some other way to find meaning in their legacy.

*"Patients can often be made more
comfortable and brought out of their
confusion with a minor drug adjustment,
giving them more control over how their
lives will end."*

# Doctors Should Help
# Terminally Ill Patients Die
# with a Clear Mind

Josh Fischman

While terminally ill patients are frequently given large doses
of drugs to help with pain and other symptoms, it should still
be possible for them to spend their last days with a clear
mind, contends Josh Fischman in the following viewpoint.
Every extra day is precious to the dying, Fischman points
out, and delirium caused by excessive medications can cause
extreme and unnecessary distress. With medication changes,
doctors can ensure that patients have control over the end of
their lives, he points out. Fischman's articles on health issues
appear frequently in *U.S. News & World Report.*

As you read, consider the following questions:

1. According to the author, while terminally ill cancer
   patients often get confused and disoriented, how often is
   this "not quite the final act"?
2. In Peter Lawlor's opinion, why is it desirable to prevent
   end-of-life delirium?
3. What did Arnie Dellinger do with his last few days of
   life, according to the author?

Josh Fischman, "Reaching Death with Comfort and a Clear Mind," *U.S. News &
World Report*, vol. 129, October 30, 2000, p. 60. Copyright © 2000 by U.S. News
& World Report, L.P. All rights reserved. Reproduced by permission.

The very worst day in her life, Sharon McCaughan recalls, was this past June 14 [2000]. It's the day she almost killed her father.

She has thought of her father dying before. Vernal Gallagher, 72, was diagnosed with prostate cancer eight years ago [in 1992], the disease has since spread to his bones. In the middle of June [2000] he began to act very confused, and McCaughan, 44, a nurse in Edmonton, Alberta, took him to the hospital. "And he went right off his nut. Started thrashing around and cursing. They put him on an IV drip of narcotics as well as sedatives and antidepressants. It hurt to watch. My dad had always tried so hard to seem so rational." And then, she says, he started losing consciousness. McCaughan and her mother agreed to continue the drugs, hoping medicine would ease him into a gentle death.

Then, perhaps because the hospital could no longer get all the drugs into his unconscious body—and drug interactions may have added to the delirium—Gallagher woke up. And he's still up. "Physically, he just wasn't ready to go. He wakes and you think, 'My God, we could have killed him with all the drugs we were using.' I had no idea delirium was common, or even that it could be reversed," McCaughan says.

It is and it can. Three quarters of terminally ill cancer patients get confused and disoriented, usually a sign that the end is near. But about half the time it's not quite the final act, according to a study published earlier this year [2000] in the Archives of Internal Medicine. Patients often can be made more comfortable and brought out of their confusion with a minor drug adjustment, giving them more control over how their lives will end.

## Not Yet Time to Go

This is tremendously important, says Peter Lawlor, a physician specializing in end-of-life care at Grey Nun's Hospital in Edmonton and coauthor of the study. "With delirium, you lose communication with the patient. He could be in more pain but unable to tell you. And a family may have traveled many miles to see him. There are issues in the past, on both sides, that they usually want to discuss. Even if you can just get a few extra days of clarity, isn't it worth it?"

Much of the confusion—for both patients and caregivers—is because drugs and a dying patient make a difficult mix. Patients are in a weakened state, and medications often have unpredictable side effects. Morphine byproducts, for instance, can reach toxic levels and affect the nervous system after the drug has been pumped into the blood for weeks. Russell Portenoy, chief of pain medicine at Beth Israel Medical Center in New York City, recalls several patients who, like Gallagher, seemed more distressed the more morphine they got. "Finally we realized what was going on, went down on the morphine, and gave them an antipsychotic. Overnight they cleared up."

## Elements of Suffering for Terminally Ill Patients

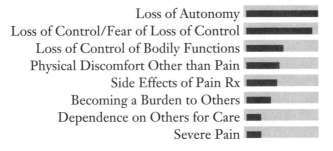

Loss of Autonomy
Loss of Control/Fear of Loss of Control
Loss of Control of Bodily Functions
Physical Discomfort Other than Pain
Side Effects of Pain Rx
Becoming a Burden to Others
Dependence on Others for Care
Severe Pain

Compassion in Dying Annual Report, 2002.

At times, switching painkillers can turn things around. In other patients the main factor may be dehydration: As they weaken they drink less, and less fluid in the body means higher drug concentrations. The way to beat this is to add water with a tiny needle just under the skin, attached to a saline drip.

"The point is that none of these are superhuman interventions. They don't require a lot," says Bertha Maloof, a nurse with the Hospice of Boston. These actions won't change the ultimate outcome, and if a patient really is close to death these simple techniques won't work. "But if they can help stop these periods of confusion, they're stopping something that's really devastating to patients and their families."

# Family Hours

Vernal Gallagher and his family are grateful for the extra months. He's going for short walks, talking to his wife, Susan, and to Sharon. "I've treasured these times," Sharon says.

This July, Arnie Dellinger, too, was fighting for time. At 55, Dellinger, a retired car salesman from South Attleboro, Mass., had been losing a battle with lung cancer, and it had spread to his brain. He was on medication to shrink the tumors. When doctors tried tapering it, Dellinger got delirious. "That was the freakiest day of my life," he recalled a few weeks after the episode. "I didn't even recognize my own granddaughter." Dellinger pushed and yelled, staggering around. "I thought it was really the end," his wife, Kathleen, remembers. But she got him to the hospital, and they started the tumor-shrinking drug again. "And the next day he was cutting the grass and gardening. It was like a miracle."

Dellinger was realistic: "There's not much doctors can do for me. But I don't want Kathleen burdened with funeral arrangements and stuff like that. So I'm taking care of it now. I was in the Army, and I want a military funeral." In late August he got his war medals polished, his dress uniform pressed, and his finances all in order.

He spent time playing with his granddaughter Haley, whom he once couldn't identify. His tasks—and his family—taken care of, Arnie Dellinger died quietly on September 6, [2000], at home.

# Periodical Bibliography

The following articles have been selected to supplement the diverse views presented in this chapter.

| | |
|---|---|
| Mercedes Bern-Klug | "The Ambiguous Dying Syndrome," *Health and Social Work*, February 2004. |
| Jane E. Brody | "A Doctor's Duty, When Death Is Inevitable," *New York Times*, August 10, 2004. |
| Jeffrey M. Drazen | "Decisions at the End of Life," *New England Journal of Medicine*, September 18, 2003. |
| Jennifer Ezel | "How Do I Deliver Hard Truths?" *Nursing*, July 2003. |
| Ian Frazier | "Everlasting," *New Yorker*, October 27, 2003. |
| Cole A. Giller | "What I Learned While Dying," *Pharos*, Summer 2003. |
| John Hardwig | "Spiritual Issues at the End of Life: A Call to Discussion," *Hastings Center Report*, March 2000. |
| Marshall B. Kapp | "The Right to Die Mad," *Pharos*, Winter 2000. |
| Colleen S. McClain, Barry Rosenfeld, and William Breitbart | "Effect of Spiritual Well-Being on End-of-Life Despair in Terminally-Ill Cancer Patients," *Lancet*, May 10, 2003. |
| Amy Rokach | "Terminal Illness and Coping with Loneliness," *Journal of Psychology*, May 2000. |
| *USA Today Magazine* | "A 'Good Death' Requires More than Medical Care," February 2001. |
| Abraham Verhese | "Hope and Clarity," *New York Times Magazine*, February 23, 2004. |
| Mark James Wilson | "Finding the Heart," *Hope*, November/ December 2002. |

# CHAPTER 4

# Should Euthanasia Be Allowed for Terminally Ill Patients?

# Chapter Preface

In the November 1994 general election, Oregon voters approved one of the most controversial ballot measures in that state's history. With 51 percent in favor and 49 percent opposed, Measure 16 was passed, establishing the Oregon Death with Dignity Act. Under the act, physician-assisted suicide became a legal option for the terminally ill. According to the law, a capable adult Oregon resident who has been diagnosed with a terminal illness by a physician may request a prescription for a lethal dose of medication for the purpose of ending his or her life. The request must be confirmed by two witnesses, and another physician must examine the patient's medical records and confirm the diagnosis. Oregon is the only U.S. state where physician-assisted suicide is legal. In 2003 forty-two terminally ill patients ended their lives under the law. According to the Oregon Department of Human Services, the majority of these people suffered from Lou Gehrig's disease, Acquired Immune Deficiency Syndrome (AIDS), and cancer.

From the beginning the Oregon law has provoked tremendous controversy as various individuals and groups have attempted to revoke or nullify it. Immediate implementation of the act was delayed by a legal injunction from Congress. After multiple legal proceedings, including a petition that was denied by the U.S. Supreme Court, the Ninth Circuit Court of Appeals lifted the injunction in October 1997, and physician-assisted suicide then became legal for terminally ill patients in Oregon. Later that year, another attempt was made to revoke the measure; Measure 51 on the general election ballot asked Oregon voters to repeal the Death with Dignity Act. Voters, however, chose by a margin of 60 percent to 40 percent to retain it. In 2003 the controversy continued as U.S. attorney general John Ashcroft attempted to suspend the licenses of doctors who prescribed life-ending medications under the Oregon law. However, in 2004 the Ninth Circuit Court of Appeals stated that Ashcroft's actions were "unlawful and unenforceable." Thus, the Oregon Death with Dignity Act continues to stand, while opponents continually mount new attacks on its legality.

Oregon is one of very few places around the world where the terminally ill can legally choose to end their lives. Belgium, the Netherlands, and Switzerland are other places where some form of euthanasia is legal; however, like Oregon, none is immune to the controversy that surrounds euthanasia. The authors in the following chapter present various opinions on whether euthanasia should be a legal option for terminally ill patients.

*"Choosing one's death is the ultimate form of liberty in any society."*

# The Terminally Ill Should Be Allowed to Choose Euthanasia

Andrea E. Richardson

The choice to end one's life is the ultimate human right, asserts Andrea E. Richardson in the following viewpoint. She believes that terminally ill patients' right to control their death must be recognized, and that doctors must learn that sometimes euthanasia helps patients more than does continuing medical treatment. Richardson is a writer from Silver Spring, Maryland. This essay received honorable mention in the 2001 *Humanist* Essay Contest for Young Women and Men of North America.

As you read, consider the following questions:

1. How have the Inuits historically ended their own lives in times of food shortages, as cited by the author?
2. In Richardson's opinion, what is the only difference between a terminally ill person and the people who threw themselves from the World Trade Center towers during the terrorist attacks of September 11, 2001?
3. According to the author, why should saving patients not be the sole measure of a physician's success?

Andrea E. Richardson, "Death with Dignity: The Ultimate Human Right?" *The Humanist*, vol. 62, July/August 2002, p. 42. Copyright © 2002 by the American Humanist Association. Reproduced by permission.

I don't ever remember a time whey my father wasn't sick. My earliest memories were of him in a hospital bed. While there were periods of time when he felt good, they were often punctuated by large setbacks that put him in the hospital for weeks at a time. My father, an executive at IBM in the 1980s, had built a good life for his family and cared deeply about his two daughters and his wife. Yet he knew that this time was limited and would probably be over before he turned forty.

## The Inevitability of Death

My father died when I was nine. He was forty-one and had outlived all of the expectations that anyone had for him. He and my mother were surprised with two children after having been told that they couldn't conceive because of the medication he had been on. They were told that any children they did have would most likely be stricken with the same disease he had—a rare form of rheumatoid arthritis [RA] that destroys not only the joints but the internal organs as well, at a young age. Both my sister and I were born healthy and, to this day, have no indication of RA. My father was told that holding down a job would be impossible, yet he managed to move to the upper executive level at IBM with little more than a high school education.

The only prediction that did come true was he died.

Death is an inevitable part of life and it is the only guarantee that we come into this world with. Eventually, our bodies will be our shortcoming. For some of us, this will happen suddenly and unexpectedly in a car or plane crash or from a sudden stroke or heart attack for which there was no obvious warning. For others—for those like my father—death is an event clearly visible on the horizon. It is an event that is forecasted, feared, and at times yearned for. For those of us who will develop terminal illnesses, death will hang ominously over our heads. Death will wage a war against the medical community. And, in the end, it is death that will be victorious.

The ability of humans to end their own lives has been around since the beginning of the species. There are stories of how at times of food shortages older Inuits would "drift away" on icebergs in order to ensure that, through their deaths, the younger members of their families would have enough food to survive. Suicide has also been proven in tribes going back thousands of years. The discovery that certain berries had lethal effects was used as a means of humane euthanasia for people who were very ill or badly injured.

## A Narrow View of Medical Care

The morality of much of the medical establishment hasn't evolved to take into account the quality of life for those who are dying. Whether a doctor sits quietly by at a patient or family's request and doesn't treat a disease or injury (passive euthanasia) or whether a physician administers a lethal dose of medication at a patient or family's request (active euthanasia), it is the doctor who is held accountable for the death of that individual. The medical establishment's narrow view of there being only one way to handle the dying patient—by using every last resource available to try to save her or him—has greatly hindered the quality of our deaths. Physicians are trained to believe that they have done their job only if every last measure is taken, regardless of what value this saps from the patient's quality of life. This is the model by which the medical establishment measures its success.

What is needed is a paradigm shift in the educational curriculum of medical schools. No one can place value on what any individual considers to be "quality of life" because we all have different bodily functions that we consider more important than others. What one person considers an extraordinary means of intervention, another may see as typical. Furthermore, what is extraordinary at one point in history isn't necessarily extraordinary at another time.

Just seventy years ago, the invention of insulin to treat diabetes was considered a major breakthrough. Today, millions of people are administrated insulin daily to treat diabetes, and few of us would call this treatment extraordinary (though it should be noted that there are some religions which do consider routine interventions of this kind extraordinary and strictly forbidden). When my father ultimately succumbed in 1988 to kidney failure as a result of his RA, kidney transplants were somewhat extraordinary and were available for only a very few select patients. Today, kidney transplants are common and often successful.

At this point in time, extraordinary covers treatments such as ventilators, high-risk surgery with low chance of success, feeding tubes, and multiple organ transplants. It is when people are placed in situations requiring any of these that they and their families often wonder whether the treatment is worth the extra time and pain when, instead, they could die a "natural" death.

---

## Control, Not Pain, Is at Core of "Right to Die" Movement

Most people . . . choose doctor-aided death not to avoid pain, but to exert autonomy. . . .

They want it in increasing numbers.

In 1947, when a Gallup survey asked Americans if the law should allow doctors to end the lives of terminally ill patients who request such assistance, 37 percent said yes and 54 percent said no. In 1999, 61 percent said yes and 35 percent said no, revealing a significant historical shift. . . .

In February [2000], an article in the *New England Journal of Medicine*, examined an Oregon Health Division study of the 33 people who requested and received lethal medications in 1999. It came to this emphatic conclusion: "The patients requested assistance with suicide because of concern about loss of autonomy and control of bodily functions, not because of concern about inadequate control of pain."

Mark O'Keefe, *San Diego Union-Tribune*, March 24, 2000.

---

A large part of the dying process revolves around the issue of control. Like so many others, I watched in horror on September 11, 2001, as people threw themselves to their deaths from the World Trade Center towers [after the towers were damaged by a terrorist attack]. The ability to choose how to end their lives in such a situation was their way of controlling the situation. The only difference between them and a terminally ill person is that the people in the World Trade Center had the physical ability to end their lives and were, at the time, free from legal intervention to prevent them from doing so. They chose to die with dignity rather than wait for death to consume them.

## A Complex Solution

A solution to the dilemma of dying by passive or active euthanasia is a complex one. First, there has to be a dialogue with the medical community and the legal community about what can be done to free physicians from prosecution should they be asked to assist a patient in dying. The appropriate measures need to be in place to ensure safety of everyone involved.

Second, there needs to be an established measure for each terminally ill patient and her or his family as to what they determine "extraordinary" and what they consider "ordinary." Currently there seems to be very few physicians who are willing to engage in this dialogue, and those who will are subject to the peer pressure of the general medical establishment.

Finally, there needs to be shift in the way physicians are educated. Saving the patient shouldn't be the sole measure of a physician's success. While this is an easy yardstick, since life is a tangible and measurable occurrence when contrasted to death, there should be a higher standard of success based upon following the specific wishes of a patient and his or her family. While this can be a little more ambiguous than the black and white "life or death," it will allow for better medical treatment and will ensure that more people are dying the way they desire to.

When a person is terminally ill, it seems only natural that the benefits of prolonging life should be carefully weighed. While I don't believe that one physician should be solely in charge of making this decision, I do believe that euthanasia—whether passive or active—should be determined by a roundtable discussion that includes the patient (if possible), the attending physicians, and any close family members.

Death is the last thing that we do in this world, so it makes sense that it should occur with as much dignity as our civilized society can allow. While the medical establishment has made striking advances in its treatment of human ailments, we must recognize that progress takes time and eventually we all must die. Choosing one's death is the ultimate form of liberty in any society and something that will remain at the forefront of discussion until each of us has the right to die as we wish.

| "*To legalize euthanasia would damage important, foundational societal values and symbols that uphold respect for human life.*"

# The Terminally Ill Should Not Be Allowed to Choose Euthanasia

Margaret Somerville

In the following viewpoint Margaret Somerville argues that individuals should not be allowed to choose euthanasia because it would be harmful to both society and the medical profession. Euthanasia cannot be simply a matter of personal choice, she contends, because it would destroy one of the most important foundations of society—a prohibition on killing. She also points out that for society to maintain faith in physicians, doctors must not have the power to kill people. Somerville is Gale Professor of Law and professor in the faculty of medicine at the McGill University Centre for Medicine, Ethics, and Law in Montreal, Canada.

As you read, consider the following questions:
1. How does Somerville define euthanasia?
2. As explained by the author, how is euthanasia a "gene machine" response to human life?
3. According to Somerville, of the people who requested assisted suicide under Oregon's Death with Dignity Act, what percentage changed their minds after receiving pain relief treatments?

Margaret Somerville, "The Case Against Euthanasia and Physician-Assisted Suicide," *Free Inquiry*, Spring 2003, pp. 33–34. Copyright © 2003 by the Council for Democratic and Secular Humanism, Inc. Reproduced by permission.

There are two major reasons to oppose euthanasia. One is based on principle: it is wrong for one human to intentionally kill another (except in justified self-defense, or in the defense of others). The other reason is utilitarian: the harms and risks of legalizing euthanasia, to individuals in general and to society, far outweigh any benefits.

When personal and societal values were largely consistent with each other, and widely shared because they were based on a shared religion, the case against euthanasia was simple: God or the gods (and, therefore, the religion) commanded "Thou shalt not kill." In a secular society, especially one that gives priority to intense individualism, the case for euthanasia is simple: Individuals have the right to choose the manner, time, and place of their death. In contrast, in such societies the case against euthanasia is complex.

## Definitions

Definitions are a source of confusion in the euthanasia debate—some of it deliberately engendered by euthanasia advocates to promote their case. Euthanasia is "a deliberate act that causes death undertaken by one person with the primary intention of ending the life of another person, in order to relieve that person's suffering." Euthnasia is not the justified withdrawing or withholding of treatment that results in death. And it is not the provisions of pain relief, even if it could or would shorten life, provided the treatment is necessary to relieve the patient's pain or other serious symptoms of physical distress and is given with a primary intention of relieving pain and not of killing the patient.

## Secular Arguments Against Euthanasia

1. *Impact on society.* To legalize euthanasia would damage important, foundational societal values and symbols that uphold respect for human life. With euthanasia, how we die cannot be just a private matter of self-determination and personal beliefs, because euthanasia "is an act that requires two people to make it possible and a complicit society to make it acceptable." The prohibition on intentional killing is the cornerstone of law and human relationships, emphasizing our basic equality.

Medicine and the law are the principal institutions that maintain respect for human life in a secular, pluralistic society. Legalizing euthanasia would involve—and harm—both of them. In particular, changing the norm that we must not kill each other would seriously damage both institutions' capacity to carry the value of respect for human life.

To legalize euthanasia would be to change the way we understand ourselves, human life, and its meaning. To explain this last point requires painting a much larger picture. We create our values and find meaning in life by buying into a "shared story"—a societal-cultural paradigm. Humans have always focused that story on the two great events of each life, birth and death. Even in a secular society—indeed, more than in a religious one—that story must encompass, create space for, and protect the "human spirit." By the human spirit, I do not mean anything religious (although this concept can accommodate the religious beliefs of those who have them). Rather, I mean the intangible, invisible, immeasurable reality that we need to find meaning in life and to make life worth living—that deeply intuitive sense of relatedness or connectedness to others, the world, and the universe in which we live.

There are two views of human life and, as a consequence, death. One is that we are simply "gene machines." In the words of an Australian politician, when we are past our "best before" or "use by" date, we should be checked out as quickly, cheaply, and efficiently as possible. That view favors euthanasia. The other view sees a mystery in human death, because it sees a mystery in human life, a view that does not require any belief in the supernatural.

Euthanasia is a "gene machine" response. It converts the mystery of death to the problem of death, to which we then seek a technological solution. A lethal injection is a very efficient, fast solution to the problem of death—but it is antithetical to the mystery of death. People in post modern societies are uncomfortable with mysteries, especially mysteries that generate intense, free-floating anxiety and fear, as death does. We seek control over the event that elicits that fear, we look for a terror-management or terror-reduction mechanism. Euthanasia is such a mechanism: While it does not al-

153

low us to avoid the cause of our fear—death—it does allow us to control its manner, time, and place—we can feel that we have death under control.

Research has shown that the marker for people wanting euthanasia is a state that psychiatrists call "hopelessness," which they differentiate from depression—these people have nothing to look forward to. Hope is our sense of connection to the future; hope is the oxygen of the human spirit. Hope can be elicited by a sense of connection to a very immediate future, for instance, looking forward to a visit from a loved person, seeing the sun come up, or hearing the dawn chorus. When we are dying, our horizon comes closer and closer, but it still exists until we finally cross over. People need hope if they are to experience dying as the final great act of life, as it should be. Euthanasia converts that act to an act of death.

Asay. © by Charles Asay. Reproduced by permission.

A more pragmatic, but nevertheless very important, objection to legalizing euthanasia is that its abuse cannot be prevented, as recent reports on euthanasia in the Netherlands have documented. Indeed, as a result of this evidence some former advocates now believe that euthanasia cannot be safely legalized and have recently spoken against doing so.

To assess the impact that legalizing euthanasia might have, in practice, on society, we must look at it in the context in which it would operate: the combination of an aging population, scarce health-care resources, and euthanasia would be a lethal one.

2. *Impact on medicine.* Advocates often argue that euthanasia should be legalized because physicians are secretly carrying it out anyway. Studies purporting to establish that fact have recently been severely criticized on the grounds that the respondents replied to questions that did not distinguish between actions primarily intended to shorten life—euthanasia—and other acts or omissions in which no such intention was present—pain-relief treatment or refusals of treatment—that are not euthanasia. But even if the studies were accurate, the fact that physicians are secretly carrying out euthanasia does not mean that it is right. Further, if physicians were presently ignoring the law against murder, why would they obey guidelines for voluntary euthanasia?

Euthanasia "places the very soul of medicine on trial." Physicians' absolute repugnance to killing people is necessary if society's trust in them is to be maintained. This is true, in part, because physicians have opportunities to kill not open to other people, as the horrific story of Dr. Harold Shipman, the British physician–serial killer, shows.[1]

How would legalizing euthanasia affect medical education? What impact would physician role models carrying out euthanasia have on medical students and young physicians? Would we devote time to teaching students how to administer death through lethal injection? Would they be brutalized or ethically desensitized? (Do we adequately teach pain-relief treatment at present?) It would be very difficult to communicate to future physicians a repugnance to killing in a context of legalized euthanasia.

Physicians need a clear line that powerfully manifests to them, their patients, and society that they do not inflict death; both their patients and the public need to know with

---

1. In 2000, Shipman was convicted of killing fifteen of his patients; however, it is widely believed that he killed more than a hundred.

absolute certainty—and to be able to trust—that this is the case. Anything that would blur the line, damage that trust, or make physicians less sensitive to their primary obligations to protect life is unacceptable. Legalizing euthanasia would do all of these things.

## Euthanasia Is Wrong

Euthanasia is a simplistic, wrong, and dangerous response to the complex reality of human death. Physician-assisted suicide and euthanasia involve taking people who are at their weakest and most vulnerable, who fear loss of control or isolation and abandonment—who are in a state of intense "pre-mortem loneliness"—and placing them in a situation where they believe their only alternative is to be killed or kill themselves.

Nancy Crick, a sixty-nine-year-old Australian grandmother, . . . committed suicide [in 2002] in the presence of over twenty people, eight of whom were members of the Australian Voluntary Euthanasia Society. She explained: "I don't want to die alone." Another option for Mrs. Crick (if she had been terminally ill—an autopsy showed Mrs. Crick's colon cancer had not recurred) should have been to die naturally with people who cared for her present and good palliative care.

Of people who requested assisted suicide under Oregon's Death with Dignity Act, which allows physicians to prescribe lethal medication, 46 percent changed their minds after significant palliative-care interventions (relief of pain and other symptoms), but only 15 percent of those who did not receive such interventions did so.

How a society treats its weakest, most in need, most vulnerable members best tests its moral and ethical tone. To set a present and future moral tone that protects individuals in general and society, upholds the fundamental value of respect for life, and promotes rather than destroys our capacities and opportunities to search for meaning in life, we must reject euthanasia.

*"The ability to demand physician aid in dying is the only resource dying patients have with which to 'send a message' . . . to physicians."*

# Legalizing Euthanasia Empowers Patients and Improves Quality of Care

Richard T. Hull

In the following viewpoint Richard T. Hull makes the case that legalizing euthanasia would help ensure that the terminally ill receive adequate end-of-life care, and would give them more control over the way they die. In his opinion, patients, not doctors or the government, should have the right to decide when death is appropriate. Hull is professor emeritus of philosophy at the State University of New York at Buffalo, and editor of the book *Ethical Issues in the New Reproductive Technology.*

As you read, consider the following questions:
1. Why do many physicians fail to order adequate narcotics for the terminally ill, in Hull's opinion?
2. According to the author, to which physicians should the power of assisted-suicide be restricted?
3. What is the doctrine of double effect, as explained by Hull?

Richard T. Hull, "The Case for Physician-Assisted Suicide," *Free Inquiry*, Spring 2003, pp. 35–36. Copyright © 2003 by the Council for Democratic and Secular Humanism, Inc. Reproduced by permission.

In early 1997, the medical community awaited the U.S. Supreme Court's decision in *Vacco v. Quill*. Ultimately, the high court would overturn this suit, in which doctors and patients had sought to overturn New York's law prohibiting physician-assisted suicide. But it was fascinating to see how much attention physicians suddenly paid to the question of pain management while they were waiting.

Politicians and physicians alike felt shaken by the fact that the suit had made it as far as the Supreme Court. Medical schools scrutinized their curricula to see how, if at all, effective pain management was taught. The possibility that physician-assisted suicide would be declared as much a patient's right as the withdrawal of life-sustaining technology was a clarion call that medicine needed to "houseclean" its attitudes toward providing adequate narcotics for managing pain.

## The Only Way to "Send a Message" to Physicians

The ability to demand physician aid in dying is the only resource dying patients have with which to "send a message" (as our public rhetoric is so fond of putting it) to physicians, insurers, and politicians that end-of-life care is inadequate. Far too many patients spend their last days without adequate palliation of pain. Physicians sensitive to their cries hesitate to order adequate narcotics, for fear of scrutiny by state health departments and federal drug agents. Further, many physicians view imminent death as a sign of failure in the eyes of their colleagues, or just refuse to recognize that the seemingly endless variety of tests and procedures available to them can simply translate into a seemingly endless period of dying badly. Faced with all this, the ability to demand—and receive—physician aid in dying may be severely compromised patients only way to tell caregivers that something inhumane stalks them: the inhumanity of neglect and despair.

Many physicians tell me that they feel it is an affront to suppose that their duty to care extends to a duty to kill or assist in suicide. If so, is it not even more an affront, as dying patients and their families tell me, to have to beg for increases in pain medication, only to be told that "We don't want to make you an addict, do we?" or that "Doctor's orders are being followed, and Doctor can't be reached to revise them." If apologists for the status quo fear that a slippery slope will lead to voluntary euthanasia, then nonvoluntary euthanasia, the proponents of change already know that we've been on a slippery slope of inadequate management of suffering for decades.

Let's examine some of the stronger arguments against physician-assisted suicide—while keeping in mind that these arguments may not be the deepest reasons some people oppose it. My lingering sense is that the unspoken problem with physician-assisted suicide is that it puts power where opponents don't want it: in the hands of patients and their loved ones. I want to see if there are ways of sorting out who holds the power to choose the time and manner of dying that make sense.

## Empowering Patients Through Choice

1. *Many severely compromised individuals, in their depression, loneliness, loss of normal life, and despair, have asked their physicians to assist them in dying. Yet later (after physicians resisted their requests and others awakened them to alternative opportunities) they have returned to meaningful lives.*

No sane advocate of physician-assisted suicide would deny the importance of meeting the demand to die with reluctance and a reflective, thorough examination of alternative options. The likelihood of profound mood swings during therapy makes it imperative to distinguish between a patient's acute anguish of loss and his or her rational dismay at the prospect of long-term descent into the tubes and machines of intensive care.

But note that, in stories like the above, it is the very possibility of legal physician-assisted suicide that empowers patients to draw attention to their suffering and command the resources they need to live on. Patients who cannot demand to die can find their complaints more easily dismissed as "the disease talking" or as weakness of character.

## Medicine Would Not Suffer

2. *Medicine would be transformed for the worse if doctors could legally help patients end their lives. The public would become distrustful, wondering whether physicians were truly committed to*

# The Right to Choose Death

Evelyn was diagnosed with breast cancer in 1997. She spent the next four years dying.

At first she waged war on the cancer, attacking her own body with radiation and pills until she was left inhabiting something limp and unresponsive. Still, the cancer continued to grow inside her, replicating through her spine, shoulders, hips, pelvis, and liver.

She watched as her body began to fail her. There were awful waves of pain, violent coughing, constipation, abdominal cramps, convulsions, and humiliation. She had trouble breathing and walking. The sickness was overwhelming her. Evelyn was moved to an assisted living facility, where she was told she had less than six months to live. Plastic tubes were strung up, around and through her body. She lay on her hospital bed like a wax figure. There was nothing heroic about barely persisting.

Evelyn had seen her mother die a horrible, cringing death. She did not want that for herself. She wanted to die with dignity. On September 24, 2001, Evelyn asked the hospice nurse to help end her life. The nurse provided her with a number of Compassion in Dying, a nonprofit organization that supports the right of terminally ill patients to hasten their deaths. It agreed to help.

Evelyn thought about having her family and medical personnel with her as she ended her life. This made her happy. On November 27, 2001, she swallowed a glass of liquid medication, slipped immediately into a coma, and died fifteen minutes later, at the age of seventy-two. Two days earlier, she had written a letter: "On Thanksgiving, I hope everyone in my family will take time to feel thankful that I live in Oregon and have the means to escape this cancer before it gets any worse. I love you all."

Lawrence Rudden, *World & I*, May 2003.

---

saving lives, or if they would stop striving as soon as it became inconvenient.

Doubtless there are physicians who, by want of training or some psychological or moral defect, lack the compassionate sensitivity to hear a demand for aid in dying and act on it with reluctance, only after thorough investigation of the patient's situation. Such physicians should not be empowered to assist patients to die. I would propose that this power be restricted to physicians whose primary training and profession is in pain management and palliation: they are best equipped to ensure that reasonable alternatives to euthanasia and suicide are exhausted. Further, patients appeals for assisted suicide should be scrutinized by the same institutional ethics committees that already review requests for the suspension of life-sustaining technology as a protection against patient confusion and relatives' greed.

## A Personal Judgment

3. *Euthanasia and physician-assisted suicide are incompatible with our obligations to respect the human spirit and human life.*

When I hear *all* motives for euthanasia and physician assisted suicide swept so cavalierly into the dustbin labeled Failure to Respect Human Life, I'm prompted to say, "Really? *Always?*" Those same opponents who find physician-assisted suicide appalling will typically excuse, even acclaim, self-sacrifice on behalf of others. A soldier throws himself on a grenade to save his fellows. A pedestrian leaps into the path of a truck to save a child. Firefighters remain in a collapsing building rather than abandon trapped victims. These, too, are decisions to embrace death, yet we leave them to the conscience of the agent. Why tar all examples of euthanasia and physician-assisted suicide with a common brush? Given that we do not have the power to ameliorate every disease and never will, why withhold from individuals who clearly perceive the financial and emotional burdens their dying imposes on loved ones the power to lessen the duration and extent of those burdens, in pursuit of the values they have worked to support throughout their lives?

Consider also that some suffering cannot be relieved by any means while maintaining consciousness. There are individuals, like myself, who regard conscious life as essential to personal identity. I find it nonsensical to maintain that it is profoundly morally *preferable* to be rendered comatose by drugs while awaiting life's "natural end," than to hasten death's arrival while still consciously able to embrace and welcomes one's release. If I am irreversibly comatose, "I" am dead; prolongation of "my life" at that point is ghoulish, and I should not be required to undergo such indignity.

Finally, the question, "What kind of life is worth living?" is highly personal. There are good reasons patients diagnosed with a wide range of conditions might not wish to live to the natural end of their diseases. How dare politicians and moralists presume to make these final judgments if they don't have to live with the results? Of course, every demand for physician-assisted suicide must be scrutinized, and determined to be fully informed. To withhold aid in dying beyond that point is, first, barbarically cruel. Second, it only increases the risk that individuals determined to end their lives will attempt to do so by nonmedical means, possibly endangering others or further magnifying their own suffering.

## A Matter of Simple Justice

4. *The time-honored doctrine of double effect permits administering pain-relieving drugs that have the effect of shortening life, provided the intent of the physician is the relief of the pain and not the (foreseen) death of the patient. Isn't that sufficient?*

Others may find comfort in the notion that the intention of the agent, not the consequences of his or her action, is the measure of morality. I do not. In any case, preferences among ethical theories are like preferences among religious persuasions: no such preference should be legislated for all citizens. For the thinker who focuses on consequences rather than intentions, the fact that we permit terminal care regimens to shorten life *in any context* shows that the line has already been crossed. The fact that physicians must, at the insistence of the competent patient or the incompetent patient's duly appointed surrogate, withdraw life-sustaining technology shows that physicians *can* assist patient suicides and can perform euthanasia on those fortunate enough to be dependent on machines. It becomes a matter of simple justice—equal protection before the law—to permit the same privileges to other terminal patients. That the U.S. Supreme Court has ruled against this argument did not dissuade the citizens of the State of Oregon from embracing it. States like New York that have turned back such initiatives must bear the shame of having imposed religious majorities' philosophies on all who suffer.

*"Contrary to the expectations of euthanasia proponents, legal sanction [of euthanasia] empowers physicians—not patients."*

# Legalizing Euthanasia Eliminates Patient Autonomy and Reduces Quality of Care

Herbert Hendin

Legalizing euthanasia would not empower terminally ill patients, argues Herbert Hendin in the following viewpoint. Instead, he contends, it would give more power to doctors and lead to the killing of patients without their full consent. Hendin advocates better pain relief to help the terminally ill enjoy a good quality of life and die a good death. Hendin is medical director of the American Foundation for Suicide Prevention and professor of psychiatry at New York Medical College. He coauthored *The Case Against Assisted Suicide: For the Right to End-of-Life Care.*

As you read, consider the following questions:

1. What did the 1990 and 1995 studies of euthanasia in the Netherlands reveal, according to Hendin?
2. As cited by the author, how many Dutch physicians stated that they had terminated the lives of patients without an explicit request from the patient to do so?
3. According to Hendin, what does the situation in Oregon reveal about palliative care when euthanasia is legal?

Herbert Hendin, "Assisted Suicide, Euthanasia, and the Right to End-of-Life Care," *Crisis: The Journal of Crisis Intervention and Suicide Prevention*, vol. 23, 2002, pp. 40–41. Copyright © 2002 by Hogrefe & Huber Publishers, www.hhpub.com. Reproduced by permission.

D oes our need to care for people who are seriously or terminally ill and to reduce their suffering require us to permit physicians to end these patients' lives?

Awareness of the inadequacies of the care we provide to those who are dying makes it not surprising that if people are asked: "Are you in favor of euthanasia?" a majority reply that they are. Further questioning reveals, however, that they mean little more than that they would rather die painlessly than die painfully. When people are asked: "If terminally ill, would you rather be given treatment to make you comfortable or have your life ended by a physician?" their responses are quite different.

What most people do not know is that such relief is now possible. Having experienced the painful death of a family member or friend, many assume it is not. When a knowledgeable physician addresses the desperation and suffering that underlie the request for assisted suicide and assures the patient that he or she will continue to do so until the end, most patients change their minds, no longer want to hasten death, and are grateful for the time remaining to them. But at this time only a minority of patients receive such care.

## Better Care Is Needed for the Terminally Ill

In varying degrees compassion for suffering patients and respect for patient autonomy serve as the basis for the strongest arguments in favor of legalization. Compassion, however, is no guarantee against doing harm. A physician who does not know how to relieve a patient's suffering may compassionately (but inappropriately) agree to end that patient's life. Patient autonomy is an illusion when physicians do not know how to assess and treat patient suffering, and the choice for patients becomes continued agony or a hastened death. Only recently have we recognized the need to train general physicians in how to relieve the suffering of terminally ill patients. It is not surprising that studies show that the more physicians know about palliative care, the less they favor assisted suicide or euthanasia; the less they know, the more they favor it.

Opposition to legalization in the United States is strongest among physicians who know the most about caring for terminally ill patients, i.e., palliative care specialists, gerontologists, psychiatrists who treat patients who become suicidal in response to medical illness, hospice physicians, and oncologists. They know that patients requesting a physician's assistance in suicide are usually telling us as strongly as they know how that they are desperate in their need for relief from their suffering, and that without such relief they would rather die. They are making an anguished cry for help and a very ambivalent request to die. When treated by a physician who can hear their ambivalence, understand their desperation, and relieve their suffering, the wish to die usually disappears. For the small number with intractable symptoms, sedation at the end of life can at least insure a painless death.

## Euthanasia Empowers Doctors, Not Patients

What happens to autonomy and compassion when assisted suicide and euthanasia are legally practiced? With 20 years' experience, the Netherlands, the only country in which assisted suicide and euthanasia have had legal sanction, provides the best laboratory to help us evaluate what they mean in actuality. I was one of three foreign observers to have had the opportunity to study the situation in the Netherlands extensively and to discuss specific cases with leading Dutch practitioners as well as interview Dutch government-sponsored euthanasia researchers about their work. All three of us independently concluded that the guidelines established by the Dutch for the practice of assisted suicide and euthanasia—a competent patient who has unrelievable suffering makes a voluntary request to a physician, who before going forward must consult with another physician and afterwards must report the case to the authorities—were consistently violated and could not be enforced.

Concern over charges of abuse led the Dutch government to undertake studies of the practice in 1990 and 1995. Many violations of the guidelines were evident from these two studies. For example, 60% of Dutch cases of assisted suicide and euthanasia are not reported, which by itself makes regulation impossible.

The most alarming concern to arise from the Dutch studies has been the documentation of several thousand cases a year in which patients who have not given their consent have their lives ended by physicians. About a quarter of physicians stated that they had "terminated the lives of patients without an explicit request" from the patient to do so, and a third more of the physicians could conceive of doing so.

## Compassion or Abandonment?

People who support assisted suicide believe they are being compassionate. But are they really?

Imagine having a terminal illness and despairing about becoming a burden to your family, or of being forced to die in agony. You go to your doctors and suggest that perhaps the answer is assisted suicide. The doctor shrugs and says, "Well, it's your choice." Wouldn't that confirm your worst fears about the value of your life, your future prospects for suffering, your concern that you are now a burden on your family?

Assisted suicide is not an answer to the problems it seeks to address; it is to surrender to them. If we wish to remain a truly compassionate society that cares deeply for our ill, disabled, elderly, and dying, we will reject the siren song of killing and focus intently on improving care and suicide prevention to help the suicidal ill and disabled overcome the desire to end their lives.

Wesley J. Smith, *Free Inquiry*, Spring 2003.

The evidence of the Dutch experience also indicates that contrary to the expectations of euthanasia proponents, legal sanction empowers physicians—not patients. Physicians often suggest death, which compromises the voluntars of the process; they are not aware of or do not present obvious alternatives; they ignore patient ambivalence; and they even end the lives of patients who have not requested their doing so. Practicing euthanasia appears to encourage physicians to think they know best who should live and who should die, an attitude that leads them to make such decisions without consulting patients. One case presented to me as requiring euthanasia without consent involved a Dutch nun who was dying painfully of cancer. Her physician felt her religion prevented her from agreeing to euthanasia so he felt both justified and compassionate in ending her life without telling her he was doing so.

Given legal sanction, euthanasia, originally intended for the exceptional case, has become an accepted way of dealing with serious or terminal illness in the Netherlands. In the process, palliative care has become one of the casualties, while hospice care has lagged behind that of other countries. In testimony before the British House of Lords, Zbigniew Zylicz, a medical oncologist who specializes in palliative medicine and is one of the few palliative care experts in the Netherlands, attributed Dutch deficiencies in palliative care to the easier alternative of euthanasia.

For anyone inclined to believe that assisted suicide could be implemented in the United States in some way that avoids the problems seen in the Netherlands, careful study of the situation in Oregon—the one state in the country that has legalized assisted suicide (but not euthanasia)—provides evidence to the contrary. Under the Oregon law, when a terminally ill patient makes a request for assisted suicide, physicians are required to point out that palliative care and hospice care are feasible alternatives. They are not required, however, to be knowledgeable about how to relieve either physical or emotional suffering in terminally ill patients. Without such knowledge the physician cannot truly present feasible alternatives. It would seem necessary that if lacking such training a physician should be required to refer any patient requesting assisted suicide for consultation with a physician knowledgeable about palliative care. There is, however, no such requirement in the Oregon law. The few Oregon cases of which details are known reveal that adequate palliative care options were not given; patient depression and incompetence were ignored, as was pressure applied by relatives.

## Better Care for the Dying Is Needed

The Oregon and Dutch experiences provide convincing evidence that legalization of assisted suicide and euthanasia undermines the care provided to patients at the end of life. The challenge we face is to create a culture that identifies the care of the seriously ill and dying as a public health issue. There needs to be a strong social commitment to both respecting the dignity and individuality of dying patients and their families, and providing them with real choices for real care at the end of life. As we do so the issue of whether to legalize assisted suicide and euthanasia is likely to become irrelevant.

*"There remains a serious gap between the choices people want at the end of their lives and what they are now permitted."*

# Physician-Assisted Suicide Should Be Legalized

Faye Girsh

In the following viewpoint Faye Girsh argues that physician-assisted suicide is favored by the majority of society and should thus be legalized. According to Girsh, advances in medical science have eradicated many diseases that kill suddenly, and instead death is frequently a prolonged and painful process for many people. Patients have a right to choose to end that suffering, she maintains, even if it means physicians must help them to die. Girsh is the former president of the Hemlock Society, a right-to-die organization based in Denver, Colorado, now called End-of-Life Choices.

As you read, consider the following questions:

1. Of the people who die every year, what type of illnesses do 90 percent suffer from, as cited by the author?
2. What does the legalization of assisted suicide in Oregon reveal about what terminally ill people want, according to Girsh?
3. Without the reassurance that someone will be there to help them, what do terminally ill patients often do, according to the author?

Faye Girsh, "Death with Dignity: Choices and Challenges," *USA Today*, March 2000. Copyright © 2000 by the Society for the Advancement of Education. Reproduced by permission.

While Americans consider themselves free to live the lives they choose, most don't realize that this freedom ends when it comes to selecting a peaceful death over a life filled with unbearable pain and suffering. Euthanasia advocate Jack Kevorkian's conviction of second-degree murder for assisting in the nationally televised suicide of terminally ill Thomas Youk has shown that, despite achieving great legal successes over the last 25 years, Americans have a long way to go in securing the freedom to die with dignity when confronted by terminal illness.

## Living Longer

Interest in the right-to-die issue has become increasingly important as people are now enjoying longer, healthier lives than at any time in history. Diseases that kill suddenly and prematurely have been virtually wiped out in developed countries. What are left are conditions that often result in lingering, agonizing declines—cancer, stroke, Parkinson's disease, and amyotrophic lateral sclerosis (Lou Gehrig's disease), to name a few. Ninety percent of the people who die each year are victims of prolonged illnesses or have experienced a predictable and steady decline due to heart disease, diabetes, or Alzheimer's disease.

Medicine can keep people alive with artificial organs, transplants, and machines—even artificial food and water—rather than allowing a terminally ill patient a quick death through pneumonia or organ failure. Modern medicine often does more than prolong living—it actually extends dying.

A study of dying patients in five major medical centers revealed that 59% would have preferred to receive just care to make them more comfortable, instead of the aggressive treatment they got. Another study surveyed Canadian patients who identified five areas of importance at the end of life: receiving adequate pain and symptom management; avoiding prolonged dying; achieving a sense of control; relieving the burden on loved ones; and strengthening relationships with people.

A big advancement in caring for terminally ill patients has come with the growth in hospice care, which started with one facility in 1974 and has grown to almost 3,000 nationwide, making it accessible to most Americans. Hospice care is designed to control pain and provide physical and spiritual comfort to those who are dying. It neither prolongs nor hastens death. While hospices have dramatically improved end-of-life care, there remains a serious gap between the choices people want at the end of their lives and what they are now permitted.

## When Life Is Not Worth Living

Living is not merely breathing. It's not living as we know it when the ability to communicate is no longer with us, when the love of those close to us has turned to pity, and when waking up simply means another day to be lived in pain.

We who have been making hard decisions for so many years must have the right to make that final decision, the hardest one of all.

Keith Taylor, *Free Inquiry*, Spring 2003.

Patients' rights at the end of their lives take two forms—the right to refuse medical treatment when faced with inevitable death and the right to secure a doctor's help in ending suffering at the end of life. It took the deaths of two young women—Karen Ann Quinlan and Nancy Cruzan—to give every American the right to make medical decisions in advance. Both had gone into irreversible comas following accidents and, after lengthy legal battles, their parents received permission from the courts to disconnect their daughters' life support.

In Cruzan's case, which took place 14 years after Quinlan's, the Supreme Court ruled that every American has the right to refuse unwanted medical treatment for any reason, even if it leads to death. This includes the right to refuse food and fluids. Justice William Brennan wrote, "Dying is personal. And it is profound. For many, the thought of an ignoble end, steeped in decay, is abhorrent. A quiet, proud death, bodily integrity intact, is a matter of extreme consequence."

## Dying in Oregon

Physician-assisted dying is legal today only in Oregon, where voters legalized the practice in 1994 and again in 1997. During the first year, 23 patients obtained medication from their doctors, but just 15 used it to end their lives. Six others died natural deaths, and two were still living when the study was completed. This shows that people want to know they have a choice, but not all will take advantage of it. Under the provisions of the Oregon Death with Dignity Act:

- The request must come voluntarily from a mentally competent, terminally ill, adult resident of Oregon.
- Two physicians must examine the patient to confirm the diagnosis and prognosis.
- A mental health professional must be consulted if either doctor has a question about mental competence, depression, or coercion.
- All other alternatives must be presented and explained to the patient.
- The patient must make witnessed requests orally and in writing.
- After a 15-day waiting period, the patient receives a physician's prescription for a lethal dose of medication, which can be filled following a two-day waiting period.
- All prescriptions under the Death with Dignity law must be reported to the state health department.
- The patient is then free to take the medication when and if he or she wishes. Family, friends, and a doctor may be present.

## More Control

Thanks to the laws allowing patients to refuse medical treatment and the growing availability of hospice care, we have more control over how we die. The changes happened because people demanded better care and more options at the end of life. These progressive measures were opposed at first because of the fear of abuse. Naysayers predicted that giving individuals the choice to live or die would lead to a cheapening of human life. Now, though, they don't have to have treatment they don't want and can rely on someone they select to speak for them when they can't. They can refuse additional treatment, opt for hospice care, and hasten their death by refusing food and water. These choices work to give the terminally ill more control, but they still haven't gone far enough.

In a survey of 30,000 Americans over the age of 55, 65% said that people with a terminal illness should have a legal right to hasten their death with a doctor's assistance. Carol Poenisch, the adult daughter of a woman with Lou Gehrig's disease who ended her life with the help of Kevorkian, described her mother's condition in the *New England Journal of Medicine*. Her mother could not speak, support her head, or swallow. Extreme weakness meant she required help to do everything. When she discovered that Kevorkian could help her die, she made that choice. According to her daughter, "She was much more at ease with her illness and her death than I. She was much braver about it, and she was calm." Her mother's decision was not unusual for people suffering from this debilitating disorder—56% of patients with Lou Gehrig's disease say they would consider making the same choice.

After three operations for lung cancer, a 62-year-old woman could hardly breathe and suffered suffocating chest pain. Although hospice care helped with her symptoms, she was ready to die. She contacted the Hemlock Society, which provides information and support for a peaceful death. Through the Caring Friends program, a trained volunteer worked with her and her husband to ensure that she had exhausted all the alternatives, that she knew the right way to end her life, and that a medical professional was in attendance when she died. The woman found a compassionate physician who, risking his license and liberty, supplied her with the right amount of lethal medication. She died peacefully, in the company of her husband, best friend, and a Caring Friends volunteer. Because this woman lived in a state where assisting a death is illegal, everyone involved, including the Hemlock Society, could have been subject to prosecution.

## Why Involve Doctors?

Why is it necessary to involve doctors? Why can't people just kill themselves? In this country, suicide is not a crime. However, suicide, as it traditionally is thought of, involves violence, uncertainty, and pain for the family. Some terminally ill people end their lives while they can, often prematurely, fearing there will be no way to do it if they wait too long. Without the reassurance that someone would be there to help, people often commit suicide violently and use the wrong methods, which can traumatize their loved ones in the process.

Austin Bastable, a Canadian man with multiple sclerosis, who died with the help of Kevorkian, said, "Knowing that such dedicated people exist, I could afford to live longer than I originally had planned—because I knew that I no longer had to rely solely upon my limited abilities to end my life." Those with terminal illnesses should be able to die peacefully, gently, quickly, and with certainty—in the arms of people they love. This requires medical assistance.

Let's consider a typical case, that of Rose, an 82-year-old woman with terminal pancreatic cancer. She has made peace with her dying and receives care at home from a hospice nurse. She is on a morphine pump to control her pain, although she dislikes being sedated. Weak, tired, and nauseated, she knows the end is near and begs for a quick, peaceful death. Her children want to help her, but, because aiding her to die is against the law, they can only watch while she suffers.

Many people, like Rose's children, have cared for a loved one who wants to die, but cannot get the assistance to make it happen. Asking someone for help to die, or being asked to help, is not only emotionally difficult, it could lead to breaking the law.

This tortuous situation occurs every day. If she were hooked up to some kind of treatment, Rose could legally and easily request that it be stopped and she could die, but she isn't. So her children must stand by when their mother is begging them to help her die, and they have to continue to watch her suffer.

Except in Oregon, the law does not allow the family to work with a terminally ill patient's doctor to help end his or her suffering. Some physicians in other states break the law and provide assistance; some family members try to help, but don't know how, and the attempt fails tragically. The patient and the family should be able to discuss their end-of-life choices with their doctor and explore all other alternatives, but be able to know there will be aid in dying if the situation is hopeless and the request persistent.

Each of us needs to make plans to ensure that the end of life remains in our control. Just as we write wills to dispose of our worldly goods, we can make decisions about what medical treatment is acceptable and what is not. You can write a living will, which says you do not want drastic measures taken if you have no hope for recovery. You can choose a person to make your health care decisions if you are unable to. (This is called the Durable Power of Attorney for Health Care or Health Care Proxy.) That individual should be someone you trust, who knows what you want, and will fight for your rights.

If you agree that physician aid in dying should also be a choice for terminally ill, mentally competent adults who request it, there are things you can do:

- Join an advocacy organization, such as the Hemlock Society, that supports legal change.
- Tell your state and national representatives how you feel.
- Vote if there is an initiative in your state.
- Discuss the issue with your family, doctor, and spiritual advisor.

How you die should be your choice. As poet Archibald MacLeish said, "Freedom is the right to choose: the right to create for yourself the alternative of choice. Without the possibility of choice and the exercise of choice, a man is not a man but a member, an instrument, a thing."

*"Doctors have a special responsibility to show by word and deed, in season and out, that intentionally killing another person is simply wrong."*

# Physician-Assisted Suicide Should Not Be Legalized

Lawrence Rudden and Gerard V. Bradley

In the following viewpoint Lawrence Rudden and Gerard V. Bradley argue that a physician should never kill a terminally ill patient, even if that patient wants to end his or her life. The medical profession must be based on respect for life, assert Rudden and Bradley, with no exceptions. In their opinion, patient autonomy never includes the right to demand death from a physician. Rudden is director of research for the Graham Williams Group in Washington, D.C. Bradley is professor of law at the University of Notre Dame, Indiana.

As you read, consider the following questions:
1. According to the authors, what is the special responsibility of doctors?
2. For what reason might it be acceptable for a doctor to prescribe a toxic dose of painkillers, according to Rudden and Bradley?
3. In the authors' opinion, why are our feelings unreliable guides to making sound decisions?

Lawrence Rudden and Gerard V. Bradley, "Death and the Law—Why the Government Has an Interest in Preserving Life," *The World & I*, vol. 18, May 2003, p. 255. Copyright © 2003 by News World Communications, Inc. Reproduced by permission.

A ttorney General [John] Ashcroft wants to stop doctors who kill. He has good reason: doctors have a special responsibility to show by word and deed, in season and out, that intentionally killing another person is simply wrong. Yes, even if that person is, like Evelyn, terminally ill.[1]

## Doctors Should Never Kill

A doctor's calling is always to heal, never to harm. A doctor's calling is special, though not unique. None of us possesses a license, privilege, or permission to kill, but the healer who purposely kills puts into question, in a unique way, our culture's commitment to the sanctity of life. The scandal created by doctors who kill is great, much like that caused by lawyers who flout the law, or bishops—shepherds—who do not care about their flocks. Whenever someone whose profession centers upon a single good—healing or respect for law or caring for souls—tramples that good, the rest of us cannot help but wonder: is it a good after all? Maybe it is for some, but not for others? Who decides? Is all the talk of that good as supremely worthwhile idle chatter or, worse, cynical propaganda?

## Importance of Respecting Life

Do not intentionally kill. This is what it means—principally and essentially—to revere life. Making intentional killing of humans a serious crime is the earmark of society's respect for life. All our criminal laws against homicide (save for Oregon) make no exception—none whatsoever—for victims who say they want to die. Our law contains no case or category of "public service homicides," of people who should be dead. People hunting season is never open. Our laws against killing (except Oregon's) make no exception for those who suffer, even for those near death. None.

When someone commits the crime of murder, all we can say is that the victim's life was shortened. We know not by how much; the law does not ask, or care. After all, no one knows how much longer any of us shall live. Many persons

---

1. Evelyn, a seventy-two-year-old Oregon resident dying of cancer, ended her life in 2001 through physician-assisted suicide.

who are the picture of health, in the bloom of youth, will die today in accidents, by another's hand, or of natural causes. Yes, we can say with confidence that someone's death, maybe Evelyn's, is near at hand. But so long as she draws breath, she has the same legal and moral right that you and I have not to be intentionally killed.

## Difference Between Intending and Accepting Death

It is not that life is the only good thing which we, and our laws, strive to protect. Life is not always an overriding good; we accept certain risks to life. What is the alternative? Do nothing at all that creates some (even a small) chance of death? Would we get up in the morning? Drive our cars? Take medicine? Go swimming? Fly in airplanes? Some risk to life is acceptable where the risk is modest and the activities that engender it are worthwhile.

Sometimes the risk can be great and still worth accepting. We might instinctively step in front of a car, or jump into a freezing lake to save a loved one, or a stranger's wandering toddler. We might do the same upon reflection, but we do not want to die. We do not commit suicide.

Religious martyrs may face certain death, but they do not want to die. They submit to death as the side effect of their acts, whether these be described as witnessing to the truth, or, in the case of Saint Thomas More, avoiding false witness.[2] The axman, the lion tamer, the firing squad—they kill. They intend death.

This distinction between intending and accepting death is not scholarly hairsplitting. This distinction is real, as real as space shuttles. The *Columbia* crew knew all along that they risked death by flying into space.[3] That which they risked came to be, but they were not suicides.

Of course doctors may—even must—prescribe analgesics. Doctors should try to relieve the suffering of their terminal patients, up to and even including toxic doses. Not because

2. More was beheaded in 1535 after refusing to take an oath to King Henry VIII.
3. In February 2003 the space shuttle *Columbia* burst into flames after reentering the atmosphere, killing everyone aboard.

they want to kill, any more than they want to kill patients in exploratory surgery. Doctors who prescribe strong painkillers want to help, even to heal. Given how ill some patients are, the risk of death is worth running, just as some very risky surgeries are a risk worth taking.

## Follow the Money

It takes only about forty dollars for the drugs used in an assisted suicide. But it could take $40,000 (or more) to provide the medical care and mental health support necessary to alleviate an ill or disabled person's suicidal desire. In a health care world dominated by health maintenance organizations (HMOs), where profits come from cutting costs, assisted suicide would ultimately be about money.

Wesley J. Smith, *Free Inquiry*, Spring 2003.

Evelyn wants to let go, and she needs help to do so. Yet, none of us walks into a doctor's office and demands a certain treatment. Doctors do not fetch medicines upon demand. They are not workmen at our service. Yes, doctors work toward our health in cooperation with us. They have no right to impose treatment we do not want. But we have no right to drugs, surgery, or anesthesia.

Or to lights out—even for Evelyn.

## Life Is a Common Good

Why? Because autonomy, or self-rule, is not an all-consuming value. It is not a trump card. Evelyn honestly wishes to bring down the curtain. We may find her condition hideous, as she evidently does, but our feelings (of repulsion, sympathy, or whatever) are unreliable guides to sound choosing. Feelings certainly do not always, or even usually, mislead us. Often, though, they do.

Pause a moment and you will, if you try, think of something attractive and pleasing you did not choose today, because it would have been wrong, and something unappealing, even repulsive, you chose to do because it was right. For me, some days, it has to do with my mother, who suffers from advanced Alzheimer's. Enough said.

On what basis does a society and its governing authorities

decide that life is a great common good? Because it is true: life is good. The law is a powerful teacher of right and wrong. Like it or not, what our laws permit is thought by many to be good, or at least unobjectionable. What the law forbids is believed to be, well, forbidden.

Why should our government take such an unyielding stand in favor of life? Because we are all safer where everyone's life is prized, not despised.

*"Legal or not, euthanasia happens all the same. . . . Far better to bring it into the light, and develop a more rigorous . . . procedure for dealing with [it]."*

# Euthanasia Should Be Legalized and Regulated by the Government

*Economist*

Despite being illegal in most countries, euthanasia happens anyway, according to the editors of the *Economist* in the following viewpoint. Because of this, and the fact that citizens in a democracy have a right to end their lives if they choose, the editors argue that euthanasia should be legalized so that it can be regulated. By legalizing and properly regulating the practice, the editors point out, the terminally ill can be protected from botched suicide attempts and greater suffering. The *Economist* is a British newspaper that publishes analysis of world business and current affairs.

As you read, consider the following questions:
1. Why did Diane Pretty and her husband go to court, as explained by the author?
2. What is the "slippery-slope" argument against terminal illness, according to the *Economist?*
3. What is needed to ensure that only those who have completely thought it through are eligible for euthanasia, according to the author?

Nobody chooses the hour of his birth, but many would like a say in the manner and timing of their death. A good end is one in which an individual is ready to die and can retain as much control as possible over the whole process, supported by loved ones and able to leave life with both dignity and privacy.

This is what Diane Pretty, a British woman with a fatal degenerative condition called motor neurone disease, wants to do, by committing suicide. But because her illness has left her paralysed, she needs assistance to do it. Although English law permits suicide, it punishes those who aid and abet it. So Mrs Pretty's lawyers went before the House of Lords this week [November 17, 2001] to argue that it should overturn an earlier appeals-court ruling and allow her husband to help her to commit suicide without fear of subsequent prosecution.[1]

## Arguments Against Assisted Suicide

There are strong arguments against this sort of assisted suicide, whether it takes the form of the withdrawal of life-sustaining treatment or of more active measures such as the administration of lethal injections. Many people object to it on moral or religious grounds. Some doctors believe that it violates their ethic to "do no harm" and that it would further undermine an already fragile doctor-patient relationship. Others worry that people who cannot afford expensive care may see no alternative to their predicament other than suicide. And there is also the slippery-slope argument: once assisted suicide is permitted for the terminally ill, vulnerable members of society, such as old people regarded as a nuisance by their families, may all too easily be pushed down it.

## Arguments for Legalisation

But the arguments for legalising assisted suicide are stronger. Democracy rests on the right to self-determination, so long as it does not compromise the welfare of others. People like Mrs Pretty, who are nearing death with their minds intact but their bodies falling apart, have a right to end their lives in as humane a way as possible. The alternative of "do-it-yourself"

1. The Prettys lost their case. Diane died at a hospice in May 2002.

euthanasia can lead to botched attempts and greater suffering, much as "backroom" abortions once did.

## No Evidence for the "Slippery Slope" Argument

|  | 1998 | 1999 | 2000 |
|---|---|---|---|
| Lethal prescriptions written: | 24 | 33 | 39 |
| Patients who took lethal dose*: | 16 | 27 | 27 |
| Median age of those who died: | 70 | 71 | 69 |
| Married patients who took lethal dose: | 2 | 12 | 18 |
| Patients referred for psychiatric evaluation: | 5 | 10 | 5 |
| Those whose underlying illness was cancer: | 14 | 17 | 21 |
| Physicians who prescribed lethal dose: | 14 | 22 | 22 |
| Median length of patient-physician relationship (weeks): | 11 | 22 | 8 |
| Median interval between first oral request and death (days): | 22 | 83 | 30 |
| Physicians present when ingested: | 8 | 16 | 14 |

*In both 1999 and 2000, one of the 27 patients who died was prescribed the lethal medication in the previous year.

"Oregon's Death with Dignity Act: Three Years of Legalized Physician-Assisted Suicide," Dept. of Human Services, Oregon Health Division, Center for Disease Prevention and Epidemiology, February 22, 2001.

The medical technology that has successfully prolonged Mrs Pretty's life to this stage also offers the most humane means of ending it. What is needed in such cases is a robust system of medical and psychiatric assessment, along with counselling, to ensure that only those who have completely thought it through are eligible for assisted suicide. The Netherlands, which legalised euthanasia earlier this year [2001], requires patients who want it to gain the approval of two doctors, and it also has a formal assessment procedure after the fact. Oregon, whose more restricted system of assisted suicide is now under attack by the federal government, has even more hurdles in place. This may seem over-bureaucratic, but, since suicide is irreversible, it is better to err on the side of caution.

Although voluntary euthanasia should be permitted, it

should be only part of a broader, better system of dealing with death, including improved pain-management and psychological support. Legal or not, euthanasia happens all the same, with doctors quietly colluding with patients and their families, and the occasional case dragged before the courts. Far better to bring it into the light, and develop a more rigorous and transparent procedure for dealing with an increasingly common fact of modern life.

*"What I cannot stomach is the idea of applying to the state for a licence . . . to kill or be killed."*

# Euthanasia Should Not Be Legalized and Regulated by the Government

Matthew Parris

In the following viewpoint Matthew Parris maintains that no responsible government can assume the authority of legalizing and regulating euthanasia. Parris believes that the role of the government should be to protect life above all else. Making decisions about life and death are too important to be left to the determination of any type of government regulatory body, argues Parris. Parris is a political columnist for the daily British *Times* newspaper.

As you read, consider the following questions:
1. Why did Reginald Crew travel to Switzerland, as explained by the author?
2. Why does Parris believe that euthanasia is different from "the right to die"?
3. According to the author, for those contemplating euthanasia, why may contemplation of losing the law's protection not be an inappropriate hurdle to clear?

Sometimes one's creed points logically where one is intuitively reluctant to go. The flesh is willing but the spirit is weak. Item: we should not give money to women begging with babies as this only encourages them. Item: this is a beggar and she is carrying a baby. Conclusion: . . . er . . . fumble in pockets for change. (She just looked so wretched.)

One settles such conflicts by following a hunch. This is not necessarily the triumph of unreason. We should never question the primacy of reason, but we cannot always be sure what reason dictates. Sometimes the heart may guess early at reasons which the brain proves slower to recognise. Sound argument should be paramount, yes, but sometimes intuition is early warning of an argument that is not as sound as it seems.

## The Death of Reginald Crew

And so it happened that, libertarian to my boots, I thought I would be in favour of what euthanasia campaigners call the Right to Die until this week [January 2003] BBC [British Broadcasting Corporation] 1's *The Morning Show* asked me to do a turn on their sofa to discuss Mr Reginald Crew's plan (he is now the late Mr Reginald Crew) to travel to Switzerland where he could be assisted to kill himself. Mr Crew, who was 74, had been suffering for four years from motor neurone disease; there was no cure, his deterioration was remorseless, and life had become (he said) no longer worth living.

An action which causes another person's death, even at his request, is unlawful in Switzerland as it is here, but the Swiss have been more flexible in their prosecution policy and tend to turn a blind eye to the work of reputable and humane organisations such as Dignitas, the group that assisted Mr Crew by giving him poison to drink through a straw. Though his impunity in Switzerland was assured, it is not clear to me that this would have been a crime even here in Britain where we adhere as unbendingly as we can to the distinction between failing to resuscitate or prolong life, which is not usually a crime, and actively taking life, which usually is. This is a blurred and difficult frontier to police; prosecution is not the invariable rule, conviction does not always follow, and, if it does, sentences are usually lenient or even derisory. But the line is more or less held.

After agreeing to appear on *The Morning Show*, I sat down quietly and thought my libertarianism through. I knew intuitively that I admired Mr Crew and might well have done the same were I in his dilemma. But should he have had to go to Switzerland to face it?

## Two Means to Reform

It appeared to me that if we sought the kind of reform which would have assisted Mr Crew, two alternative means were available. We could make 'He asked me to' a defence to murder and have done with it, leaving judges and juries to determine case by case whether the accused really had satisfied himself that his victim was of sound mind and had formed the settled desire to have himself killed. But I saw, too, that, appealingly simple though (to a libertarian) this might be, it would never do. We cannot go around killing anyone who asks us to, however emphatically. The law would additionally want to know that the accused had made a reasonable attempt to satisfy himself that the victim's wish was well founded, that the accused had no ulterior motive, that he knew and understood the victim, that the victim had had all that was needful drawn to his attention, that. . . .

And I could see where, in Britain at least, the case for reform must tend: to the alternative of setting up a Euthanasia Commission composed of expert persons competent to decide applications for death. Killing people cannot be left to private initiative, the killer subsequently making the best defence he can to any putative murder charge. The proposal would have to be considered in advance by some sort of adjudicating body.

## Giving People the Right to Kill

For let us be clear that killing people is what is under discussion. The late Mr Crew went to Switzerland to have poison poured down his throat. It is not quite honest to call this 'assisted suicide' and disingenuous to speak, as the euthanasia lobby do, of 'the right to die'. We already have the right to die. Suicide has not been a crime [in the United Kingdom] for some half a century. The need for euthanasia arises when the victim lacks the means or power to take his own life and can only request (on the instant or in advance by some sort of letter of intent) that someone else take his life. The euthanasia lobby wish to give that person the right to kill.

## The Dutch Example

In February 1993, after 15 years of agitation by a vocal, pro-death minority, the members of the Dutch Parliament saw no reason to continue the contradiction between their nation's laws and actual practice. They legalized what was "happening anyway," allowing for doctor-assisted death in "extreme circumstances." These were loosely defined in the words of the Royal Dutch Medical Association's own euthanasia guidelines.

Some view the 1993 Dutch law as "pioneering legislation," but the social consequences have been devastating. The "right" to die mutates swiftly into an "obligation" for those who are too much of a burden on society. Four out of five nursing homes in Holland have closed since 1980. The elderly have become an endangered underclass, afraid to seek medical treatment. Doctors and nurses, on the other hand, find themselves above the law, a more powerful elite than any aristocracy of old.

Michael J. Miller, *Wanderer*, December 14, 2000.

If you hand me a dagger and say, 'I am too weak to do it; here, plunge this between my ribs,' I take it you are asking me to kill you. If I comply, and am discovered, my discoverer will cry, 'You killed him!' and I will reply, 'Yes, but he asked me to.' What difference in principle is there between this and the less bloody alternative in which (say) you indicate a phial of poison and say, 'I am too weak to drink this; here, raise it to my lips and pour it down,' or, 'Inject me with this'? No question about it: you ask me to kill you.

I am not in principle against killing people. In a just war, in self-defence, as a means of preventing greater killing, or even (at times) in overwhelming sympathy for another's suffering, it is something we may contemplate. But to take another's life in peacetime is an enormous step, perhaps the most enormous. If there is anything which should not be done lightly or without anguish, this is it. For those who contemplate such an action, to be forced—at least to contemplate losing the law's protection may not be an inappropriate hurdle to expect them to clear. I can think of worse tests of good faith than to ask that the killer love his victim enough to risk arrest for killing him.

I will kill myself if I ever have to, and I may. I would break the law and kill a friend if I ever had to—and face the consequences. But what I cannot stomach is the idea of applying to the state for a licence, to be issued upon the determination of an appointed regulatory body, to kill or be killed. If one man's Right to Die gives another the Right to Kill, and if the Right to Kill means giving the government the right to withdraw Permission to Live, then give me prison.

# Periodical Bibliography

The following articles have been selected to supplement the diverse views presented in this chapter.

| | |
|---|---|
| *Christianity Today* | "Death by Default," February 5, 2001. |
| Len Doyal and Lesley Doyal | "Why Active Euthanasia and Physician Assisted Suicide Should Be Legalised: If Death Is in a Patient's Best Interest Then Death Constitutes a Moral Good," *British Medical Journal*, November 10, 2001. |
| Tom Flynn | "The Final Freedom: Suicide and the 'New Prohibitionist,'" *Free Inquiry*, Spring 2003. |
| Herbert Hendin | "The Practice of Euthanasia," *Hastings Center Report*, July/August 2003. |
| Nat Hentoff | "It's Not Only About Terri Schiavo: Barriers to Killing Come Down," *Village Voice*, November 26–December 2, 2003. |
| Stephen Kiernan | "It's My Life, It's My Decision," *Burlington Free Press*, September 8, 2004. |
| Michael J. Miller | "Deluge of Death in Netherlands?" *Wanderer*, December 14, 2000. |
| Anna Quindlen | "In a Peaceful Frame of Mind: Patients Demanding Control over Their Medical Care May Not Relinquish It in Their Final Days," *Newsweek*, February 4, 2004. |
| Lawrence Rudden | "Death and the Law," *World & I*, May 2003. |
| Thomas A. Shannon | "Killing Them Softly with Kindness: Euthanasia Legislation in the Netherlands," *America*, October 15, 2001. |
| Wesley J. Smith | "Dehydration Nation," *Human Life Review*, Fall 2003. |
| Wesley J. Smith | "Why Secular Humanism About Assisted Suicide Is Wrong," *Free Inquiry*, Spring 2003. |
| Nancy Valko | "A Lethal Evolution," *First Things: A Journal of Religion and Public Life*, December 2001. |
| Stephen Wright | "Taking Care of the Dying: While Euthanasia Sparks Heated Responses, Remember It Is a Spiritual Debate," *Nursing Standard*, August 6, 2003. |

# For Further Discussion

## Chapter 1

1. According to the report by Last Acts, America is a death-denying culture, where the majority of people do not speak or think about end-of-life care and thus have no control over the way they die. After reading the viewpoint by Lisa Miller, do you agree or disagree with this opinion? Give examples from the texts to support your answer.

2. A 2002 study found that only 15 to 20 percent of Americans have written advance directives—legal documents that specify what medical treatment can be used for a person too ill to speak for himself or herself. Both Valerie Reitman and the *Tufts University Health & Nutrition Letter* state that advance directives can be useful in making end-of-life decisions. However, Reitman maintains that these documents are frequently ignored. In your opinion, how useful are advance directives in preventing conflict over end-of-life decisions? Support your answer with examples from the texts.

3. A large number of terminally ill patients spend their last days in hospice care, where caregivers do not attempt to hasten or postpone death but simply focus on providing a high quality of life for the patient. Jack D. Gordon and Stephen Kiernan, and Gwen London present different arguments on the effectiveness of the hospice system. After reading these varying points of view, what do you believe are the benefits of hospice care? What are the dangers? What changes might improve the hospice care system?

## Chapter 2

1. Studies show that a number of terminally ill patients experience significant pain at the end of their lives that is not adequately relieved by medication. Julia Riley and Carol Sieger present two different opinions on why pain medication is not adequate for all terminally ill patients. After reading these two viewpoints, what do you think are the biggest barriers to effective pain treatment? In your opinion, what might improve end-of-life pain treatment?

2. Timothy E. Quill and Ira R. Byock advocate the use of terminal sedation to help terminally ill patients achieve a peaceful death. Mark B. Blocher contends that terminal sedation is killing and is never acceptable. Quill and Byock are medical doctors; Blocher is publisher of *Biblical Bioethics Advisor*. How does your

awareness of these authors' credentials influence your assessment of their arguments?

3. Byron Demmer argues that the seriously ill should be allowed to use marijuana to relieve their pain. Mark Souder and Janet M. LaRue contend that medical marijuana does not relieve pain and is harmful. After reading the two viewpoints, do you believe that seriously ill patients should be allowed to use marijuana? Cite from the texts to support your answer.

## Chapter 3

1. A number of the authors in chapter 3 argue that doctors do not adequately help the terminally ill die a good death. After reading their arguments, how do you think doctors might better care for terminally ill patients? Support your answer with examples from the texts.

2. Kerri Wachter maintains that doctors should speak openly with terminally ill patients about death. Do you agree with her opinion that openness can help ease the dying process? Why or why not? Use examples from the text to support your answer.

3. Myles N. Sheehan asserts that attention to spirituality is a vital part of end-of-life care. Rachel K. Sobel argues that doctor compassion is an important part of caring for the terminally ill. After reading these two viewpoints, how do you think Sheehan and Sobel might agree with one another's arguments? How might they disagree?

## Chapter 4

1. Andrea E. Richardson asserts that the choice to end one's life is the ultimate human right. Margaret Somerville argues that society's prohibition on death is more important than personal autonomy. Do you believe that people have the right to choose euthanasia? Cite from the viewpoints to back up your answer.

2. After reading the viewpoints in this chapter, how do you think legalization of euthanasia would affect the medical profession? Explain.

3. Richard T. Hull argues that legalizing euthanasia empowers patients and improves the quality of care they receive. What arguments and examples does Hull use to back up his case? In your opinion, does Hull use sufficient factual evidence to support his argument? Cite from the viewpoint to support your answer.

4. Margaret Somerville, Herbert Hendin, Lawrence Rudden and Gerard V. Bradley, and Matthew Parris all make arguments against allowing euthanasia for terminally ill patients. After reading each of these viewpoints, which author do you think makes the best argument against euthanasia? How does this author make his or her argument convincing? Which author do you think makes the least persuasive argument against euthanasia? Why?

# Organizations to Contact

The editors have compiled the following list of organizations concerned with the issues debated in this book. The descriptions are derived from materials provided by the organizations. All have publications or information available for interested readers. The list was compiled on the date of publication of the present volume; names, addresses, phone and fax numbers, and e-mail addresses may change. Be aware that many organizations take several weeks or longer to respond to inquiries, so allow as much time as possible.

**American Foundation for Suicide Prevention (AFSP)**
120 Wall St., 22nd Fl., New York, NY 10005
(888) 333-2377 • fax: (212) 363-6237
e-mail: rfabrika@afsp.org • Web site: www.afsp.org
Formerly known as the American Suicide Foundation, the AFSP supports scientific research on depression and suicide, educates the public and professionals on the recognition and treatment of depressed and suicidal individuals, and provides support programs for those coping with the loss of a loved one to suicide. It opposes the legalization of physician-assisted suicide. AFSP publishes a policy statement on physician-assisted suicide, the newsletter *Crisis*, and the quarterly *Lifesavers*.

**American Life League**
PO Box 1350, Stafford, VA 22555
(540) 659-4171
e-mail: sysop@all.org • Web site: www.all.org
The league believes that all human life is sacred. It works to educate Americans on the dangers of all forms of euthanasia and opposes legislative efforts that would legalize or increase its incidence. It publishes the bimonthly pro-life magazine *Celebrate Life*; videos; brochures, including *Euthanasia and You* and *Jack Kevorkian: Agent of Death*; and newsletters monitoring abortion- and euthanasia-related legal developments.

**American Society of Law, Medicine & Ethics (ASLME)**
765 Commonwealth Ave., Suite 1634, Boston, MA 02215
(617) 262-4990 • fax: (617) 437-7596
e-mail: aslme@bu.edu • Web site: www.aslme.org
ASLME works to provide scholarship, debate, and critical thought to professionals concerned with legal, health care, policy, and ethical issues. It publishes the *Journal of Law, Medicine, and Ethics* as well as a quarterly newsletter.

**Compassion in Dying Federation**
6312 S.W. Capitol Hwy., Suite 415, Portland, OR 97201
(503) 221-9556 • fax: (503) 228-9160
e-mail: info@compassionindying.org
Web site: www.compassionindying.org

The Compassion in Dying Federation provides information and counseling to terminally ill patients and their families about intensive pain management, comfort or hospice care, and death-hastening methods. Its members believe that terminally ill patients who seek to hasten their deaths should not have to die alone because their friends and families fear they will be prosecuted if present. Compassion in Dying does not promote suicide but sees hastening death as a last resort when all other possibilities have been exhausted. It publishes several pamphlets on intensive pain management and coping with the death of a loved one.

**Death with Dignity National Center (DDNC)**
11 Dupont Circle NW, Suite 202, Washington, DC 20036
(202) 969-1669 • fax: (202) 969-1668
e-mail: info@deathwithdignity.org
Web site: www.deathwithdignity.org

The DDNC promotes a comprehensive, human, responsive system of care for terminally ill patients. Its members believe that a dying patient's choices should be given the utmost respect and consideration. The center serves as an information resource for the public and the media and promotes strategies for advancing a responsive system of care for terminally ill patients on educational, legal, legislative, and public-policy fronts. The DDNC publishes annual reports on end-of-life issues and posts numerous articles from journals and newspapers on its Web site.

**Euthanasia Research and Guidance Organization (ERGO)**
24829 Norris Ln., Junction City, OR 97448-9559
(541) 998-1873 • fax: (541) 998-1873
e-mail: ergo@efn.org • Web site: www.finalexit.org

ERGO works to achieve the passage of laws permitting physician-assisted suicide for the advanced terminally ill and the irreversibly ill who are suffering unbearably. It seeks to accomplish its goals by providing research data, addressing the public through the media, and helping raise campaign funds. The organization helps patients to die by supplying drug information, technique advice, and moral support via e-mail or postal mail or through the manual *Final Exit*. ERGO also publishes a catalog of books and pamphlets on right-to-die topics.

**Hastings Center**
21 Malcolm Gordon Rd., Garrison, NY 10524-5555
(845) 424-4040 • fax: (845) 424-4545
e-mail: mail@thehastingscenter.org
Web site: www.thehastingscenter.org
Since its founding in 1969, the Hastings Center has played a central role in responding to advances in the medical, biological, and social sciences by raising ethical questions related to such advances. It conducts research and provides consultations on ethical issues such as assisted suicide and offers a forum for exploration and debate. The center publishes books, papers, guidelines, and the bimonthly *Hastings Center Report*.

**Hemlock Society**
PO Box 101810, Denver, CO 80250-1810
(800) 247-7421 • fax: (303) 639-1224
e-mail: hemlock@privatei.com • Web site: www.hemlock.org
The Hemlock Society believes that terminally ill individuals have the right to choose physician-assisted death to preserve their dignity and reduce suffering. The society publishes books on suicide and the dying process—including *Final Exit*, a guide for those who are suffering with terminal illnesses and considering suicide—and the quarterly newsletter *Timelines*.

**Hospice Foundation of America (HFA)**
1621 Connecticut Ave. NW, Suite 300, Washington, DC 20009
(800) 854-3402 • fax: (202) 638-5312
e-mail: jon@hospicefoundation.org
Web site: www.hospicefoundation.org
HFA advocates hospice care as an important enhancement to the American system of end-of-life care for the terminally ill. The foundation conducts research and public education programs to raise awareness of hospice programs and assist those coping with death and the process of grief. HFA publishes the monthly e-mail newsletter *HFA E-Newsletter*, and *Journeys*, a monthly newsletter to help in bereavement.

**International Task Force on Euthanasia and Assisted Suicide**
PO Box 760, Steubenville, OH 43952
(740) 282-3810
Web site: www.internationaltaskforce.org
The International Task Force on Euthanasia and Assisted Suicide is a group of individuals who oppose euthanasia. The group works to provide information on euthanasia and related end-of-life is-

sues, to promote the right of all persons to be treated with respect, dignity, and compassion, and to combat attitudes, programs, and policies that its members believe threaten the lives of those who are medically vulnerable. It conducts seminars and workshops and publishes several books on assisted suicide including *Forced Exit: The Slippery Slope from Assisted Suicide to Legalized Murder*, in addition to the bimonthly newsletter *Update*.

## National Hospice Foundation (NHF)

1700 Diagonal Rd., Suite 625, Alexandria, VA 22314
(703) 516-4928 • fax: (703) 837-1233
e-mail: nhf@nhpco.org • Web site: www.hospiceinfo.org

NHF works to educate the public about the benefits of hospice care for the terminally ill and their families. It promotes the idea that, with the proper care and pain medication, the terminally ill can live out their lives comfortably and in the company of their families. It publishes consumer brochures on hospice care including *Communicating Your End-of-Life Wishes* and *Hospice Care: A Consumer's Guide to Selecting a Hospice Program*.

## National Right to Life Committee (NRLC)

512 Tenth St. NW, Washington, DC 20004
(202) 626-8800
e-mail: nrlc@nrlc.org • Web site: www.nrlc.org

The committee is an activist group that opposes euthanasia and assisted suicide. NRLC publishes the monthly *NRL News* and the four-part position paper "Why We Shouldn't Legalize Assisted Suicide."

# Bibliography of Books

| | |
|---|---|
| Robert M. Baird and Stuart E. Rosenbaum, eds. | *Caring for the Dying: Critical Issues at the Edge of Life.* Amherst, NY: Prometheus, 2003. |
| David Barnard et al. | *Crossing Over: Narratives of Palliative Care.* New York: Oxford University Press, 2000. |
| Alexander A. Bove Jr. | *The Complete Book of Wills, Estates, and Trusts.* New York: Henry Holt, 2000. |
| Kathryn L. Braun, James H. Pietsch, and Patricia L. Blanchette, eds. | *Cultural Issues in End-of-Life Decision Making.* Thousand Oaks, CA: Sage, 2000. |
| Leighton E. Cluff | *The Lost Art of Caring: A Challenge to Health Professionals, Families, Communities, and Society.* Baltimore, MD: Johns Hopkins University Press, 2001. |
| Mark Cobb | *The Dying Soul: Spiritual Care at the End of Life.* Philadelphia: Open University Press, 2001. |
| Rachel Cohen-Almagor | *The Right to Die with Dignity: An Argument in Ethics, Medicine, and Law.* Piscataway, NJ: Rutgers University Press, 2001. |
| R.E. Erwin | *Reasons for the Fear of Death.* Lanham, MD: Rowman and Littlefield, 2002. |
| Christina Faull | *Palliative Care.* Oxford: Oxford University Press, 2002. |
| Mark Golubow | *For the Living: Coping, Caring, and Communicating with the Terminally Ill.* Amityville, NY: Baywood, 2002. |
| James Haley, ed. | *Death and Dying: Opposing Viewpoints.* San Diego: Greenhaven, 2003. |
| John Hardwig | *Is There a Duty to Die? And Other Essays in Bioethics.* New York: Routledge, 2000. |
| James M. Humber and Robert F. Almeder, eds. | *Biomedical Ethics Reviews, Is There a Duty to Die?* Totawa, NJ: Humana, 2000. |
| Jeanne Sampson Katz | *End of Life in Care Homes: A Palliative Approach.* Oxford: Oxford University Press, 2003. |
| Michael Kearney | *A Place of Healing: Working with Suffering in Living and Dying.* New York: Oxford University Press, 2000. |
| John Keown | *Regulating Voluntary Euthanasia.* New York: Cambridge University Press, 2002. |

| | |
|---|---|
| Barry M. Kinzrunner, Neil J. Weinreb, and Joel S. Policzer | *20 Common Problems in End-of-Life Care.* New York: McGraw-Hill, 2002. |
| Loretta M. Kopelman and Kenneth A. De Ville, eds. | *Physician-Assisted Suicide: What Are the Issues?* Boston: Kluwer Academic, 2001. |
| Elisabeth Kübler-Ross | *The Tunnel and the Light: Essential Insights on Living and Dying.* New York: Marlowe, 1999. |
| David Kuhl | *What Dying People Want: Practical Wisdom for the End of Life.* New York: Public Affairs, 2002. |
| Austin H. Kutscher | *Living Under the Sword: Psychosocial Aspects of Recurrent and Progressive Life-Threatening Illness.* Lanham, MD: Scarecrow, 2004. |
| Elizabeth Lee | *In Your Own Time: A Guide for Patients and Their Carers Facing a Last Illness at Home.* Oxford: Oxford University Press, 2002. |
| Erich H. Loewy | *The Ethics of Terminal Care: Orchestrating the End of Life.* New York: Kluwer Academic/Plenum, 2000. |
| June R. Lunnet et al. | *Describing Death in America: What We Need to Know.* Washington, DC: National Academies, 2003. |
| Beverly McNamara | *Fragile Lives: Death, Dying, and Care.* Philadelphia: Open University, 2001. |
| Ernest Morgan et al. | *Dealing Creatively with Death: A Manual of Death Education and Simple Burial.* Hinesburg, VT: Upper Access, 2001. |
| Richard John Neuhaus, ed. | *The Eternal Pity: Reflections on Dying.* Notre Dame, IN: University of Notre Dame Press, 2000. |
| Robert S. Olick | *Taking Advance Directives Seriously: Prospective Autonomy and Decisions Near the End of Life.* Washington, DC: Georgetown University Press, 2001. |
| Timothy E. Quill | *Caring for Patients at the End of Life: Facing an Uncertain Future Together.* Oxford: Oxford University Press, 2001. |
| Renee C. Rebman | *Euthanasia and the Right to Die: A Pro/Con Issue.* Berkeley Heights, NJ: Enslow, 2002. |
| Barbara Roberts | *Death Without Denial, Grief Without Apology: A Guide for Facing Death & Loss.* Troutdale, OR: NewSage, 2002. |

Margaret A. Somerville  *Death Talk: The Case Against Euthanasia and Physician-Assisted Suicide.* Montreal: McGill-Queen's University Press, 2002.

Lisa Yount  *Physician-Assisted Suicide and Euthanasia.* New York: Facts On File, 2000.

# Index